D0146816

THE IDEA OF POLITICAL THEORY

Frank M. Covey, Jr.
Loyola Lecture Series
in Political Analysis

RICHARD SHELLY HARTIGAN
General Editor

The Idea of Political Theory:

Reflections on the Self in Political Time and Space

TRACY B. STRONG

UNIVERSITY OF NOTRE DAME PRESS
NOTRE DAME   LONDON

© 1990
University of Notre Dame Press
Notre Dame, Indiana 46556
All Rights Reserved

Manufactured in the United States of America

Library of Congress Cataloging-in-Publication Data

Strong, Tracy B.
    The idea of political theory : reflections on the
self in political time and space / Tracy B. Strong.
        p.   cm. — (Loyola lecture series in political
analysis)
    Includes bibliographical references.
    ISBN 0-268-01168-0
    1. Political science — Philosophy.   I. Title.
II. Series.
JA71.S7953   1990
320'.01 — dc20   89-40750

320.01
S924,

258376

FOR HELENE

The earthly kingdom . . . I confess to be superflu-
ous, if the kingdom of God, as it now exists within
us, extinguishes the present life. But if it is the will
of God that while we aspire to true piety, we are
pilgrims on the earth, and if such pilgrimage stands
in need of such aids [as earthly government], then
those who take them away from man rob him of
his true humanity.

John Calvin,
Instituts de la religion chrétienne, IV, xx, 2

Contents

PREFACE

Two decades ago the Loyola Lecture Series in Political Analysis was established with the aim of fostering contemporary political philosophy through lecture presentations and their subsequent publication. During this period Loyola University Chicago has been pleased to host a distinguished company of scholars whose published lectures have enriched the literature of current political philosophy. It is a great pleasure to welcome Professor Tracy B. Strong to this company through the publication of *The Idea of Political Theory: Reflections on the Self in Political Time and Space.*

In this volume the author brings to the final, written form of his arguments the same combination of breadth and depth of analysis which characterized his lectures at Loyola in 1987. At that time, his audience was privileged to be engaged with him in an intellectual journey that was both sweeping and stimulating. Now, through this publication, that experience can be shared with an even wider audience.

I speak for everyone associated with the Lecture Series in thanking Professor Strong again for the pleasure of his company during his stay at Loyola, and for the lasting impact which his scholarship will have on all of us.

Richard Shelly Hartigan
Chicago, 1989

Acknowledgments

THE CHAPTERS of this book were originally given as The Lectures in Political Analysis at Loyola University in March and April 1987. I am deeply grateful for the invitation to Richard Hartigan, who has organized these lectures for many years, as well as to the faculty of the Loyola Political Science department, especially James Wiser, and to the audiences of the lectures.

Several of these chapters have been in my mind for many years. Chapter two was given in part as early as 1978 at the Northeastern Political Science Association Meetings. Substantial portions of chapter three were given as a paper to the Foundations of Political Theory Group at the American Political Science Association Meeting in 1975. Portions of the last chapter were given as Phi Beta Kappa and Senior Class Day lectures at Amherst College in 1978 and 1979 respectively. I thank my students there for having asked me to address them.

Over the years a number of people have read over all or part of this material. I acknowledge here with pleasure the friendship and intelligence of Benjamin Barber, Thomas Dumm, William Connolly, George Kateb, Alkis Kontos, and Robert Westman. Thanks are also due to my research assistant, Hendryck Spruyt, who read the entire manuscript with care and intelligence.

Two other voices with whom I have wrestled are present on these pages and require acknowledgment: Wilson Carey McWilliams and Stanley Cavell.

All of this material has passed through my marriage with Helene Keyssar. I am deeply grateful for her constant love, her help and participation in my struggles in and out of time and space. I dedicate this book to her.

1. Political Theory and Crisis

Wer hat uns also ungedreht, dass wir,
was wir auch tun, in jener Haltung sind
von einem, welcher fortgeht?
. . . .
so leben wir und nehmen immer Abschied.

(Who has turned us about, so that
Whatever we do, we carry the stance
Of one going away?
. . . .
Thus we live and always take our leave.)
>   Rainer Maria Rilke,
>   *Duino Elegies*, #8

No longer can the individual, as in former times, turn
to the great when he grows confused.
>   Søren Kierkegaard,
>   *The Present Age*

How Do I stand in relation to what I have been, in relation to who I am, and in relation to what I will be? What is the relation of these questions to the asking and answering of these questions by others, in the same times and spaces as I? These are the dimensions of the self. But there are many ways of answering these questions. Each set of answers might be thought of as a mode of discourse, a way of situating oneself in the world.[1] I am concerned in this book to locate and develop the understanding of the self required by that mode of discourse we recognize as politics.

The plot—I won't say the moral—of this book can be straightforwardly told: From the point of view of the understanding, a discourse can be thought of as responses to a particular set of questions. Overall a life is a set of responses to a variety of questions. The historical importance of these questions varies — at different times humans have asked certain questions rather than others. We might think of a turning figure, refracting different facets to a greater or lesser degree to a temporal and spatial variety of historical viewers. I do not want to say that human life is *constituted* by these responses. It is (perhaps merely) so understood. A life is always more than we can make of it — that is what makes it a life, and not an autobiography.[2] But a life is also for us only what we make of it and the dialectic between these two actualities allows us to try to shape who we are.

We do not and we cannot ask at the same time all questions about human life. More importantly, the questions that we ask at any one time exclude other questions but do not automatically outrank them in a given hierarchy. I am denying then that we either need or can come up with a meta-question and a meta-narrative, that is, that for human beings there is a "core" or "fundamental" understanding that tells us, once and for all, what humans beings *are*.[3] I am not sure what a reason would be which would indicate that one should choose to be *concerned* with politics, as opposed to love, friendship, religion, self-interest. Clearly, I do not, except for contingent circumstances, have to make that choice. I do know that politics is one of the most important ways that human beings have existed in organized concert with each other and themselves. I do also know — that is, I hope to show in this book — that the boundaries between the various ways in which humans have organized their lives are not clear, and that *concern* for one spills over into another.

In this sense, in that this book is about the theoretical enterprise, it is untrue to its topic. This is a book about boundary maintenance. My premise is that the mode of dealing with human relations that is politics has a particular validity, and that this validity is challenged by much that is characteristic of modernity. I want to discuss, in relation to the question of what it means to be a self or an agent, the area (not the line) of the boundaries between politics and other human activities. I want to show both why humans are tempted to move from a concern for life in politics to a life in other realms and modes, and to indicate what the costs and benefits are of retaining the political as a realm of human activity.

I take *politics* to be that form of human activity which constitutes the most general response to the simultaneous asking of the two questions, "who am I?" and "who are we?" In this, politics overlaps the other modes of discourse that make up the complexities of a life. Among these other questions we might note: "what should I do?" which I take to be the energizing question of morality; "how do I get what I want?—that of economics; "what do I want?"—one of the questions of psychology; "why do I suffer?"—the question of religion. Politics is an activity not unrelated to the answers to these other questions, but never identical to them.

The specialness of politics in our lives comes from the fact that in the acknowledgment and recognition that a "we" is a solution to the problems of the "I", we find ourselves required to live in a world which is not incoherent and which places upon us demands that, as I shall argue, we must not fulfill. We are, however, always tempted to leave the space and time of politics — its community of discourse — for other realms, with clearer boundaries, greater poise, more definition. These other realms, to which we are tempted, are three, and these three correspond to different dimensions of the self. First, the possibility and the actuality of perfection (I mean self-accomplishment) — I call this theater or drama; second, the possibility of power through knowledge — I call this science; and, third, the possibility of truth — I call this the theoretical act and see it as a way of overcoming the past. For reasons that will, I hope, become clear over the course of this book, I think of theater, science, and theory as three different responses to the query "who are you and who am I?" which, in turn, is a question necessarily related to that of "who are we?"—which I think of as the essential question of politics.

It is the glory of the political that it keeps each of these temptations constantly present to us, all the while showing us what we would lose (and gain) were we to yield to them. The question for our age — if we are, as I shall argue, in a time of epistemic transition — is what politics might look like in times to come. The danger is that we will cast politics off as useless and, so as to live unbounded, succumb to one or another of the temptations.

I wish to present *political theory* as a self-conscious community of discourse about politics. The "temptations" are other modes of discourse which I conceive as being in tension with political theory. Any human being — almost any being we recognize as human — will participate in all of these communities of discourse. The danger is that he or she will want to loosen the tension between these communities by the establishment of overly hard-edged boundaries between them. This chapter and the next three are concerned mainly with boundary drawing. The last chapter proposes an understanding of politics which responds to the exigencies of our time.

* * *

Let us start with a topic that has been both a subject matter for political theory and a source of anxiety and self-doubt. When I was in graduate school, a little over twenty years ago, we all knew that one of the questions with which we would be confronted on comprehensive exams was that of the "fact-value" debate. Could "values" be derived from "facts"? — in other words, did what we *know* about the world tell us something about what we *should do* in the world.[4] I pick this question because I will want to claim that what political theory makes available to us is neither a "fact" nor yet a "value." Nor do these distinctions apply happily to the agent which is understood and understands itself politically.

At stake was the boundary between what was "true" and hence had to be accepted and what was "right" and could thus not extend beyond the boundaries of those who held the "beliefs" in question. Much time was spent by graduate students in discussion of this topic. As we came near to the exam date, it became clear that our answers differed. We covered a wide range, from what I then saw as an unthinking positivism for which the matter was obvious to a gentle un-self-assured hermeneuticism which held that the choice of facts was a "value-laden" matter.

It was clear that this was a new state of affairs. Ten years earlier, the expected answer was a Parsonial version of Max Weber—or of what Max Weber was thought to have said. Following the translations and arguments of Talcott Parsons,[5] Weber was thought to have argued that facts were epistemologically separate from values. Social science, and by extension political science, was concerned with facts (and, in an often psychologically reductionist move, with those facts that supposedly "gave rise" to values); values were the subject matter of the less interesting parts of political theory. Concern with "values" was in some schools tolerated, in a few applauded, in many condemned.

By the time I took the comprehensive exams, the issue had hollowed itself out. It was clear that while we had to have a position on the "fact-value" question, it did not matter too much what it was. In part this was due to the self-conscious aristocratic tolerance that then reigned at Harvard. (If you were there, you deserved to be. If you deserved to be there, anything you thought, as long as you thought it in a recognizable public forum and style, demonstrated that you deserved a degree.[6]) In this particular case, it was also due to a number of intellectual and social developments that eventually served not so much to resolve the question as to remove it as a matter of concern. As far as I know, graduate students do not exercise themselves to "have an answer" to this question any more.

The fact-value question is no longer a *problem*—it does not bother us in the same way. In the course of this book I will say something more about the "fact-value problem," but I am here more interested in what happened to it. How did it happen that we moved from clarity to formalism and from there to disinterest?

The sources of this transition were several. They constitute changes in both the space and time in which the discourse of political theory took place. Since these changes are present-day matter for political theory and since they will make their appearance in diverse forms in the course of these chapters, let me rehearse them briefly. One was the seepage of Wittgensteinian and ordinary language philosophical approaches into the discussion of ethical questions.[7] Approaches differed, but what they seemed to have in common was the recognition that it was possible to speak meaningfully and come to necessary and shared conclusions about matters of value. Values were no longer the realm of subjectivity; rather they were organized forms and structures of discourse which were knowable and independent of human subjectivity. There *were* rules. This approach was pursued by a careful elaboration of the criteria which defined the space in which discourse about values could take place. Nothing required that one speak of ethics, but if one did, then one had to be speaking in such and such terms if one was to make sense at all.

The important thing is the notion of boundary-drawing. There were, it was pointed out, "two kinds of rules," one indicated what to do, the other set up what you were in fact doing.[8] A realm was delineated (some people called it a "language game") for which constitutive rules were elaborated. The standard example was by analogy to differentiate sharply between a "rule of the game" (as in "the bishop moves on the diagonal") and a "good" move in chess (you ought to castle at this point in the Ruy Lopez opening): clearly this was not a "subjective" matter. Or, examples like this were proposed: Suppose I have a watch on my wrist; it weighs five pounds and draws my arm down; it keeps pretty random time and is encrusted with obviously fake diamonds and rubies. You say: "That is not a very good watch." It won't do for me to respond that "good" is a subjective judgment and I am entitled to it. You would wonder if I knew what the words meant.[9] Just as one could establish the criteria by which a painting was a good painting, so also could one establish criteria in matters of value which removed judgment from a solipsistic subjectivity.[10] The most sensational development along these lines was Peter Winch's *The Idea of a Social Science* which argued, or at least appeared to its critics to argue, that concepts only made sense within a particular cultural context and hence that nothing could be said about a given concept except in terms of its context.[11]

If the first development consisted in part in the ordering of the world according to the terms of its constitution, a second and related development can be crystallized into the name of "Kuhn." There was a period when every graduate student doing bibliographical research for the paper his or her professor was to publish in the *American Political Science Review* seemed to come up with *The Structure of Scientific Revolutions* — a promiscuity that made one doubt if most of the assiduous bibliographers, or more likely their supervisors, had any idea of what actually happened in the book.

Kuhn, too, appeared to many readers to be reasserting the possibility that the person of knowledge could control the world through his or her knowledge of it. He seemed to indicate that the history of science, and by an unthinkingly easy extension, that of knowledge in general, was framed in terms of different paradigms, each with more or less historically defined borders, each knowable in terms of itself, each with its own rules that could be mastered. Movement between paradigms was "revolutionary" rather than incremental.

One might say that ordinary language philosophy had differentiated discourse in space into separate regions. An agent might move between them more or less at will taking care only to recognize when a boundary had been crossed — from, say, poetic discourse to moral discourse. Problems came from "category mistakes," that is, from going on holiday with language from one realm in another. Kuhn was also concerned with differentiating among different realms of discourse but instead of delineating them only in space Kuhn delineated them in time. The period in which people conversed in a Ptolemaic language gave way to the period of Newtonianism; that in turn, by a process that appeared either magical or cataclysmic, yielded to Einstein's world and discourse. History was a re-collecting of tales, hung on a set of punctuation marks. There was no clear process of cumulation.

Now Kuhn's idea was not as new as it was thought to be. As he himself recognized, it had general antecedents both in Gestalt psychology and in the work of men like R. G. Collingwood, which in turn had still more distant ancestors in the idealist thought of the nineteenth century.[12] His idea was also supported by some of the developments in ordinary language philosophy. But this time, especially in the social sciences, it "took."[13] What took, interestingly, was not the metaphor of revolution, but that of "paradigm." I shall postpone an analysis of Kuhn's actual claims to chapter three. Here we need to look at what accounts for this particular, almost paradigmatic *succes fou*, especially in the social sciences and the humanities.

To ask this question is to ask what broader cultural questions Kuhn's work was felt to provide solutions to. Any answer I give here must necessarily be painted with very large strokes, and would give a picture something like this:

The Structure of Scientific Revolutions was published in 1962. The first generation of Europeans and especially Americans whose intellectual formation was entirely post–World War II was just coming into early maturity.[14] They were dominated by the war experience, but, for the most part had not experienced it directly. Among the salient moral and intellectual questions was whether fascism might be thought of as part of or as an aberration from the rest of the Western tradition. To the degree that fascism was a logical development *of* the Western tradition, then other elements, most especially liberal democracy itself, could be potentially suspect.[15]

It is in this milieu that the notion of paradigm seemed to provide the source for an answer. To start with, Kuhn's claim about the structure of history (revolutionary shifts between paradigms) seemed to provide a way to deal with the anxieties associated with what little was left of the notion of progress after the experience of World War II. The war had made it difficult to believe in an unpunctuated liberal notion of progress and had further called into question the relation between technological development and moral behavior. In this context, the idea of a paradigm functions in a Spenglerian fashion to imply that there were simply different ways of doing things and, if East be East and West be West (and Germany, Germany) then the twain never need meet. Or, more accurately, if they did meet, there were no longer any criteria by which to compare them. In a quiet, unintended kind of way, Kuhn paradoxically allowed one to make sense both of the horrors of national-socialism *and* of the violence that now threatened to substitute for discourse between "systems" or "patterns of government," as they had revealingly come to be called. [16] This was not Kuhn's expressed intent, of course, but it is, I think, a source of his attraction.

A second reason for Kuhn's success was that in the face of moral chaos, he seemed implicitly to reassert the mastery of the great scientist. A great man could make borders and thus some kind of sense: look what Einstein had done; look what Newton had done; contrast to these giants the journeymen Michelson and Morley who failed in their experiment to determine the effect of the "ether" on the speed of light because they could not think in a revolutionary way. A *master* could find a new way of doing science — by extension, of making sense of and acting in the world — and be able (where lesser or older men could not) to see that what he was doing was now what it meant to do science. I will explore this more in chapter three, but it is important to see that for Kuhn not only did revolution uproot a normalcy, but, much more significantly, it gave rise to a period of new normalcy, different from the old.

The picture was one of possibility and it held out the zest of hope to what seemed an anti-intellectual and boring period in American society. Kuhn seemed to place a premium on youth, or at least on the ability to free oneself from the blinders that the past and the establishment imposed on one. (Again let me note that this is a sketch of what was made of Kuhn;

while he bears some responsibility for it, it is not, I think, what he meant to say.[17])

This development was reflected in, attached itself to, and formed part of a third major current which flowed around those Anglo-Americans interested in social and political theory: an interest in the new forms of discourse achieved by Marx and Nietzsche. Marx had been around for a long time, even if he had been read sparingly in the English-speaking world. When he began to read again after World War II, it was most often in a more voluntarist fashion, as a critic of the bourgeois form of life, frequently conjoined with Nietzsche, either openly or in disguise — perhaps as Antonio Gramsci.

Leaving aside the question of what they actually said, Marx and Nietzsche seemed to provide a model of a powerful theory (the emphasis is as much on "power" as it is on "theory") which legitimated both action and a kind of aristocratic subjectivism. Again the emphasis was on the rigidity of boundaries: there was "us" and "them," "slaves" and "masters," "proletarians" and "capitalists." Here also, as with Kuhn, the possibility of redemption was offered: change, radical change, was possible, even a change of the self. And here again was an answer to the recognition from World War II that, in the words of Stanley Milgram, "the disturbing possibility that human nature could not be counted on to protect us" from what "structures of power" might seek to do to us.[18]

Last, Marx and Nietzsche (and Freud, who soon joined them) seemed to tempt us with the seductive power of the ring of Gyges.[19] They allowed us to unmask the apparently most stable structures in the world and reveal them for "what they were," self-protective craven ideologies. Marx, Nietzsche, and Freud were all concerned to unearth that which could not be seen or spoken, the hidden "realities" on top of which the forms of life merely danced. And from such a dance, not just anyone could tell the dancer.[20] This was a question of liberation from the unspoken, and perhaps unspeakable, repressions which kept humans prisoner. The theorist was thus a special kind of person, in the service of freedom, struggling against that which was fetishized (Marx), totemized (Freud), or idolatrous (Nietzsche).

If, however, what has to be unmasked takes the form of a "paradigm" or, in more exalted language, an epistemic whole, then *every* aspect of that paradigm has to be unmasked. Thus, "facts" themselves went the way that "values" had gone under the assault of positivism. The very "existence" of facts was called into question. Claims to "know" facts were seen as attempts to impose ideological purity on a manifold and individual world.[21] It could not even be the case that we can preserve some aspects of bourgeois culture[22] and throw away the rest. This is one of the reasons, for instance, that revolutions had to become "cultural" and that political criticism must be so virulent and totalizing.[23]

As will become apparent later, I mean no more to approve these developments than to condemn them. Nor do I seek to "resolve" the fact-value problem. I noted with a sense of relief that none of my graduate students seem at all concerned with it: surely that reflects the beginning of the realization that whatever the difference between "facts" and "values" is, there is a distinction to be made between the two forms of statements. Without raising the question of "objectivity" we could at least say that they each rest (if that is the right word) on the different capacities of human beings.

What is important is that these developments are all related. The blurring of the boundaries between "facts and values" and the attempt to replace them with a very different set of boundaries, the relentless unmasking of everything, the pursuit of extremity in the name of liberation, the privileged position given to the theorist, all these correspond to a period in which it is increasingly difficult to find a relationship between general principles and particular events.[24] Hence the role of the theorist — to bring his or her thought into the world and make it available as flesh — is much more difficult. When some characterize these men (Marx, Nietzsche, Kuhn, others whom we will see later, like Derrida and Foucault) as "prophets of extremity,"[25] they are making an interesting mistake. All po-

litical theorists might in one sense be seen as *exponents* of extremity[26] if only because their voice is heard when they suddenly make it possible to bridge the gap between one way of
being in the world and a new one.[27] But they are not, at least
in their own terms, "prophets" as long as they act as theorists.
To be a "prophet," there would have to be an available mod-
erate center from which one would look out at the extreme.
Their claim, rather, is that the world is not as we think it to
be, and their aim is to make the world available to us as it
is. And the world as it is is already "extreme"; extremity is
thus the usual — but this denies the notion of extremity altogether. Theirs is, in part at least, "the first language for a new
set of experiences," as Nietzsche remarks. "And in that case,
simply nothing will be heard, but there will be the acoustic
illusion that where nothing is heard, nothing is there."[28]

The question is what understanding of (modern) circumstances is to prevail. In much of our political theory the twin
recognitions of death and freedom have both given us and assured us of a picture of the actor — whom we call a man, or
a self, or a person — who is roughly at one with himself, or
at least could be. Should this presupposition turn out to be
no longer true, much of the political theory that went with
it would be of diminished relevance to our times. This is an
"extreme" formulation: it is what Foucault calls the "death of
man." In humbler language, it is only the assertion that what
we mean by "human being" may have, at the most, diminished relevance.

*   *   *

I have sketched three important developments that began
to affect the Western world in the aftermath of World War
II. What was the response of political theory to these developments? There were several, but the "death of man," that is,
the crisis of the subject, was not an early focus. In order to
understand why we should deal with a crisis in the notion of
the subject, we must first look at the kinds of responses that
political theory did make in the postwar years. All of these

responses assumed the continuity of a subject for political theory, that is, of what I might call "normal politics."

In general, these responses drew their energy from the attempt to counter the so-called "behavioral revolution."[29] Responding mainly to the proposition that factual questions are separable from value questions and that the former were resolvable whereas the latter were not, "behaviorists," as proponents of a new and "more scientific" social science, had attacked the possibility of doing political theory at all. If political theory, the argument ran, purports to investigate what the good state is, then it is trying to resolve a question which simply cannot be answered. An analogy to "what flavor of ice cream should I like?" was drawn, with the clear implication that "no one can (has the right to) tell me what to like."

The intellectual foundations for the behaviorists had been laid in the logical positivism that had grown up in Europe in the early decades of the century as well as in early developments of analytic philosophy, especially in England. Unfortunately lost to behaviorism, especially in America, was the Promethean sense that had motivated early positivism.[30] In America, as positivism became behaviorism, the sense of the sin of the theoretical act against nature that had governed the Vienna Circle and even the young A. J. Ayer had been replaced by an incrementalist enthusiasm for "law-like propositions."

In any case, and whatever its human limitations, for a while this critique carried the debate. Indeed the editors of an influential series of books felt compelled to announce that political theory seemed "dead" and hoped that their work might bring about its resurrection.[31] Still, responses were not long in coming. They took several forms but all shared a common element that presupposed that it still was possible to do political theory, and that the nature of this task was not radically different from what it had been in the past.

A first set of responses, for instance, argued that the positivist critique had been based on a false conception of the difference between nature and convention. Men like Leo Strauss argued that modern thought had mistakenly abandoned "nature" in favor of convention or history.[32] Nature, as the great European political theorists from Plato onwards had presented it, must be recovered, at least by those who could. To the question of *why* moderns had determined to abandon nature, there was either no response, or, at best, hints of a dark world-historical conspiracy on the part of the "gnostics."[33]

Other responses allowed the positivist attack for all practical purposes, but suggested that as theorists we might take over developments in Anglo-American philosophy and, instead of figuring out what the good state was, figure out exactly what we *meant* by the state. The publication of George Sabine's monumental *A History of Political Theory* was an attempt to marry the new positivism into the tradition of political theory. Whereas previous commentators had taken topics such as constitutionalism as the governing thread of their historical story, Sabine rewrote the plot so as to articulate the structure of the tradition around the fact-value questions. The seminal work was perhaps T. D. Weldon's *The Vocabulary of Politics,* an attempt to determine to what political terms "properly" referred.

Much good came out of this desire for clarity. But the question of *why* it was apparently so difficult to talk of the good state was left as unaskable. More importantly, there was the assumption that "the" vocabulary of politics was given and knowable, and that a common element could be determined in all usages.

Still a third response was made in terms of the "tradition." This argued that the greats of the past had by and large identified the range of possible political responses and had, in language both striking and precise, given us the range in which our political world might vary. Furthermore, since the very elements of that tradition had become the political skeleton, if not also the flesh and blood of our modern politics, the study of the tradition would provide us with insight into the nature of the contemporary world in that it would identify the elements which made it up. This school — "Berkeley meta-

physics"—centered around the work and example of Sheldon Wolin, who with John Schaar and Norman Jacobson was
central in the formation of a generation of students at the
University of California at Berkeley. Unasked again is the
question of whether or not the modern world was radically
different in the experiences that made it possible. In that case,
the "tradition" would misdirect our intelligence.[34]

In all of these attempts, although much of merit came from
each, political theory retained a version of the idea of the person as the integral, unified, and coherent basis and focus of
the enterprise. Political theory was to locate him (and increasingly her) in a tradition, to identify those rights which per-
tained to him or her as a human being, and to find what made
him or her the thing he or she *was*. Political theory, we might
say, sought a kind of recognition scene, the production of a
moment when one would see who one (really) was. If the pe-
riphery was in motion, the task was to nail down the center.

The problem, however, was not that the center was not
holding, but that the idea of a center was itself problematic.
What can this mean?

In 1974, responding to all of these developments, William
Connolly published a collection of essays entitled *The Terms
of Political Discourse.*[35] In it, he made extensive use of an essay
by W. B. Gallie, originally published in 1956, entitled "Essentially Contested Concepts." As elaborated by Connolly, the
argument was that some concepts (like "democracy," but not
like "bachelor") were essentially contested in that they referred
to a manifold space, the dimensions of which were appraisive,
internally complex, and open. In principle, no final single resolution of what was meant by such a concept could be arrived
at without doing damage to the word as it was part of the human experience. Connolly argued that "politics" was such a
concept, not only not resolvable into its normative or its empirical aspects, but requiring a transcendence of such a dichotomy altogether. "To preserve the descriptive-normative
dichotomy by adopting a vocabulary conventionally laden with
commitments and then systematically dropping out the com-

mitments is like eating a chicken-salad sandwich without the chicken."[36]

Connolly was concerned that our analysis of politics recover the fact that politics is part of our life and that the terms which we use should neither hide nor deny that fact. On this he is to be applauded. There is a dimension in his analysis which needs further unpacking, however. Consider these sentences:

> In our politics, people engage in acts of protest and civil disobedience; they also lobby, dissent, negotiate, blackmail, vote, engage in violence, and strike. . . . [A]ny outsider who lacks our understanding of the distinctions among these actions could not possibly participate in or explain our political practices. To understand the political life of a community one must understand the conceptual system within which that life moves; and therefore those concepts that help to shape the fabric of our political practices necessarily enter into any rational account of them.[37]

This passage reflects many of the developments I have been sketching. It also brings out a central fact: these developments revolve around a claim of and to authority. For me, the key word in the above paragraph is "our." It is worth reflecting for a bit on what is entailed here.

In this paragraph, the "we" is the source of authority. Paradoxically, it is also an appeal to community. It is a claim that people who think as "we" do must necessarily come to certain conclusions, or at least a certain range of conclusions, about important political questions. Without giving a full analysis here, it is clear that this is one of the reasons that we can say a particular politics is an answer to the question "who are we?" and why political theory may be thought of as the attempt to make that answer available both esoterically and exoterically.

What is the source and nature of this authority? Upon what shared world does the "we" draw? There is a temptation to take it to mean something like "most people in our society." (I shall return to the problem of relativism in the last chapter.) This would make Connolly's position silly, and perhaps

dangerous. His appeal is rather to a community of discourse —
of ordinary language about politics, if you will.

If this is so, the "we" in Connolly is an appeal to a community, or, more precisely, it is a claim of community — seen
properly as a claim to authority. It is a claim that anyone can
make who recognizes him- or herself as a member of that community, as a person who can responsibly utter that "we."[38]

Why do I want to say that it is a claim both to community
and to authority, that the claim confounds the two? I suppose
for reasons something like these: We mean by authority that
which stands valid for a person merely because of the virtue
of the person who asserts it. Speaking of such sentiments, Emerson, in the "Divinity School Address" wrote that community is

> guarded by one stern condition; . . . it is an intuition. It
> cannot be received second hand. Truly speaking, it is not
> instruction, but provocation that I can receive from an-
> other soul. What he announces, I must find true in me,
> or wholly reject.[39]

One should note that there is no necessity that you respond
to me, that you find me in you and I the reciprocal. To find
you thus is to acknowledge you as in or on the same ground
as I. "Acknowledge" is here stronger than "agree" but is not
unrelated to it. It does not mean to find that you are just like
me, nor that we have the same "basic" characteristics or "rights";
it means to recognize — or to refuse the recognition — that we
stand on the same ground on these issues. It is best conveyed
by that moment in *King Lear* when the King, having passed
through the madness of the heath, is confronted with the
blinded Gloucester. After avoiding recognition (of himself, of
Gloucester) Lear finally yields to his humanity:

> If thou will weep my fortune, take mine eyes,
> I know thee well, thy name is Gloucester.[40]

The "intuitive" basis of authority to which Emerson draws
our attention rests on such acknowledgment. This necessarily gives it an ambiguous — "essentially contestable" — status in

that I must always find in myself that which is from another. When I am provoked — called forth — by you, in something you do or say, we two will form a community of judgment.

The answer to the question "who am I" is thus in politics also an answer to the political question of "who are we."[41] Authority and community are much closer to each other than they are often thought to be. In politics, individuality is coterminous with authority and with community. I must stand with you if I am to find you in me; likewise, there is no community without authority for when I find you in me I cannot be indifferent or disregarding. I might say that authority and community are respectively the temporal and spatial dimensions of the same lived world. I tend to speak of a relation as of "authority" when my sense of your presence in my world antedates the particular interaction. In this case, the authorizing takes precedence over presence. I tend to speak of a relation as of "community" when my sense of your presence is coterminous with my sense of my own presence; here authorization is taken for granted, and subsumed into the presence of the self to the other.

In our investigation of the source of authority contained in the "we" claims made by Connolly, we have raised the question of self-identity. Connolly can use the "we" as authoritative — that is, simultaneously assert the temporal and communal dimensions — without any trouble. To understand, however, what the force of his claim is, we must take the dimensions apart, and do theoretical damage to life as it is lived.

The question of how we stand with each other is asked at the same time as the question of how I stand to myself. But who then is the "we"? Does it mean we Americans? If so, how does this "we" come about, as I am not aware of ever having taken for myself the positions that Connolly ascribes to "us"?

Here we must be wary of answering too quickly. We have in fact posed an old, central, question of political theory. What does it mean for me (or you) to assert my (our) membership in a group to which I am not aware of ever having consented explicitly? This was the problem to which the idea of a social contract was addressed and our question reminds us of Hume's attack on the notion of the social contract, where he claims that the idea is empty since it presupposes that very thing which it hopes to establish. Hume writes famously:

> In vain we are asked in what records the charter of our liberties is registered. It was not written on parchment, nor yet on leaves or barks of trees.[42]

Hume's intention in this passage is not only to denigrate the possibility of an original contract but to assert that government cannot rest on anything like a contract (that is, on "keeping our promises") unless we are "trained in a philosophical system."[43] He suggests that the community cannot be found which is *based* on keeping its promises, unless this would be a community which rests on a particular *type* of authority, that of special training and expertise.

Hume thinks that people will only keep promises for reasons, and that they will only recognize the force of those reasons if they are trained in philosophy. Contracts — the acknowledgment of the claims of an other — are matters for *experts,* and politics is, Hume knows, too important to be left up to the experts.

Paradoxically, it is Hume's liberalism that turns him against the social contract as a basis for political society. Yet Hume has missed the point of the appeal to the contract. In part he has done so because he thinks that our knowledge of an other will only be secure if I actually *have* the sentiments to which I am claiming knowledge. Since I manifestly cannot *have* your feelings, it follows for Hume that I can only be assured of them — that you mean what you say when you promise to obey the laws, for instance — in one of two ways. First, I might be trained and skilled in detecting them — be a philosopher. If so, I *may* know if you will keep your word, although the radicalism of Hume's epistemology casts doubt on even this conclusion. If I am an ordinary person, then I can only rely on what ordinary persons rely on, what I have learned as an historical person, as, say, an Englishman. Hume's entire *History of England* is devoted to elaborating what being an English-man has come to mean. Because we cannot be philosophers, we must rely on being English, i.e., do what we have been "socialized" to do.

In the fear of losing everything, Hume has taken too much away. Hume confuses *having* with *knowing*. What the appeal to the contract is meant to establish is that for authority to be legitimate — I mean, to be *ours* — it must rest (a) on con-sent, that is, on equality and (b) that I must recognize the government as *mine*, as must you also. As noted above, any-one who acknowledges him- or herself a member of this com-munity is able to use the word "we" in the way that Connolly does and to know what they mean to say. In politics, that means (at least) that the government in question is a field in which my own identity is formed, that I must find the govern-ment in me and myself in it.

I will have worked out my concept of myself as a being in political space and time — who I am — when I am able to make and accept the "we" which is the claim to authority in these matters. I do not have to *be* you to be a "we," nor do I have to *have* your feelings, sentiments. I only have to find you in me (and likewise, you with me) for this appeal to be possible. Who I am is not given — it is precisely what is in question. Thus the legitimacy of the government is integrally bound to my sense of myself, and these in turn are bound to my sense of you and yours of me. We thus need a way to speak of com-munity and authority that makes them available to everyone, without special (professional) knowledge, and also a way to understand why we so often refuse the claim of that which is available to us. As we shall see below, these were Rousseau's concerns.

With this in mind, we must first do what Connolly does not do in his book and push the notion of essential contest-ability in another direction — perhaps I want to say "further." We need to examine the notion of the *person* that lies at the core of the "we," that is, of the criterial community on which Connolly's argument rests.

To say that the center is not holding—that there is a crisis of the self, or that "the subject is dead"—will not, by itself, do. In what way or ways is the center not holding? What is the significance of the ways in which it is not? What are the directions into which it slides? What does it mean to question the center altogether?

One way to begin in the right direction is to go back to our starting point and consider what Weber actually said about the "fact-value" distinction. Weber explores the differences and the relations between these two forms of discourse in a number of places, mostly classically, in the two essays he gave on "vocation" in Munich in 1919—"Politics as a Vocation" and "Science as a Vocation." In other words, what does it mean to act and what does it mean to know? Both essays insist first on the *theoretical* separation of what can be known from what is to be done. Take, for instance, the beginning of "Politics as a Vocation."

> This lecture, which I have to give at your request, will necessarily disappoint you in several ways. You will naturally expect me to take a position on the actual problems of the day.[44]

It is the revolutionary winter of 1918–1919. Weber finds himself at the University of Munich, before a group of students (and others: Rilke and Jaspers were in the audience also) in the heady days of the Bavarian Soviet. He is giving a lecture that we know he did not wish to deliver, yielding to the pressure from Rector Immanuel Birnbaum to give an address on "what is to be done" to an audience which desperately wanted an answer. The main thrust, he says, will be to "disappoint" them. The German is *enttäuschen,* which carries both the sense of "disappoint" and "take away illusions." But the aim of the lecture is to show the students how to be *echten Menschen,* real persons in the face of the wintry night that will come upon them.

The essay, and its companion "Science as a Vocation," insists on the double incarnation (I do not say melding) of knowledge and action in the human body. "It is a truly moving thing when a mature man, whether old or young in years, can say with all his heart and soul 'Here I stand, I can do no other.'" Then, Weber continues, the two ethics come together and such a person is, to all of those who are not "spiritually dead," a source of admiration. The characteristic of a man who accepts his vocation is responsibility for his actions, both "intellectual" and political. Likewise, the whole elaboration of the ideal type by Weber has as a central function the enforcement on the person of knowledge of the responsibility for exactly what she or he knows or does not know.[45] The point? Weber thought that all of us were "essentially contested," that we live under the sway of contradictory demands, that it was neither possible nor desirable to escape from any of these demands, and that the realization of this would enforce responsibility—no more, no less—upon us. We were to see how much we could bear, as he once remarked. After all, as Stanley Cavell comments, "only a creature that *can* judge of value *can* state a fact."[46] Our question is what kind of creature can make judgments and statements, and why should that creature be tempted in the directions I have briefly sketched out?

We are now raising the question of a person understood as a nexus of "I" and "we" as an "essentially contested concept." What are the elements of this nexus? An idea comes from St. Augustine's *Confessions.* It is an odd book, confessionally self-abnegating and condemnatory in presentation, but deeply arrogant and proud in its genesis. After all, it presumes that what a soul has to say about itself is important enough to be of interest to God, and to others. In it Augustine distinguishes between three faculties which together make up what he thinks it is to be a person.[47] The *will*, he suggests, is our faculty for shaping the future; it creates and gives form to that which will be. *Vision,* he argues, is our faculty for the present: it lets us see others and in turn be seen by them; it is the basis of the reciprocity which is the foundation of politics. And *memory* is our faculty for shaping and having a past. All three of these faculties are together determinative of the self. They define a space that the mystery of time incarnates as a person. They lie under thought and reason, and make them possible.

Over the course of this book I shall attempt to deconstruct the self along these lines, suggesting that there is a tension between them. In vision, we are tempted to theatricalize our self; in will, the scientific temptation is to remove oneself from the world of which one is a part. In the perversion of memory that is the attempt at theoretical self-assuredness, we seek to be immaculate, untouched by the world. To all of these, the response will be that of limitation, not needing to pose questions we cannot answer.

*   *   *

One contribution of the late Michel Foucault to political thought comes in his analysis of the notion of a person. Foucault distinguished two past periods during which what it meant to be a self was quite different from what he thinks the future holds.[48] In the first of these, which he calls "classical," that which was essential to a human being was in principle part of an infinite; our experiences here on earth were only examples of limitation in relation to this infinity. Hence, in Foucault's terms, that which makes up a human being was not the human form but the form of God. In a real manner of speaking, "man" was not the epistemological basis of the world since the world was understood in terms of the relations that existed between human beings and the infinite. For example, as Foucault analyzes in *Les mots et les choses,* in this *episteme* one sought the "character" of a living being, the "root" of language, and money (or soil) was understood as the defining core of wealth.[49]

As we move into the nineteenth century changes occur. As well as anything else this moment is marked by Hegel in section 124 of the *Philosophy of Right,* where he asserts that "the pivot and center of the difference between antiquity and modern times is the right of the subject's particularity, his right to be satisfied, or in other words the right of subjective freedom." Hegel refers to this as a "new form of civilization" and argues that the self, now conceived of as particular entity, enters into relations with other outside forces.[50] It is no longer the infinite but now the forces of the finite — life, work, and language. This is the period that sees the rise of biology, political economy, and linguistics.

For Foucault, however, and in difference from Hegel, it is not only the case that "man becomes conscious of his finiteness"; even more, it is that in confronting and then becoming conscious of his finiteness, that "man" becomes a reality. If the nineteenth century is the century of "man," it is because the human being is defined now against finite external forces. Just as the world now comes to be seen as a source of limitation, so also does work now simply produce a particular entity, no longer something which defines the quality of a human being.[51] Foucault has moved beyond the point which Hegel and Marx identified as the importance of labor, where labor gave the definition of the human being.[52]

From this, the next move is obvious. It would consist in asking if the form of civilization characteristic of "man" (the nineteenth century, as Hegel and Marx described it) were being replaced by another. In such a change nothing would strike us any longer as the expression and satisfaction of human desire and intention. And, as Nietzsche notes in the beginning of *Zarathustra,* humans would no longer know that they lacked anything. If what it means to be a human being is defined by the transformation of the relation of forces that make up a person at one time in response to changing sets of forces which are "outside" him or her, what are the consequences of the change of the outside in the period following the nineteenth century? As Foucault recognizes, Nietzsche is the first to have seen this. The central question for Nietzsche is not the question of the death of God — that was, as Nietzsche himself wrote, an *altgermanisches Wort* — it was rather the question of the permanent guarantee of the identity of the "person" in the period following the death of God.[53]

Much as I neither wished to praise nor to condemn the developments in social science, I do not wish to welcome or denounce the possibility of what Foucault calls "the death of man."[54] What I do wish to do here is to explore the temptations that human beings — at the limit of his or her time — are open to in relation to politics. We saw above that some of the important developments in the practice of political theory responded to needs for boundary-drawing, for the empowering of theory or at least of the status of theory. I want to move towards an exploration of why those developments occurred — to what did they respond in our present condition.

This book is written with the sense of a time of crisis — at what one might call a liminal point in human history. It is worth taking some space here to say what this means and to indicate to what arguments it is opposed.

This crisis is not "merely" an intellectual one — as if the mind were necessarily as separate in all of us as some pretend it is in them. Take for an instance the column by George Will in the *International Herald Tribune* of January 23rd, 1987, entitled "There is No 'Right Way' to Rent a Human Womb." After arguing with some forcefulness that one cannot make "womb rental" harmless and that all such contracts that subordinate nature and responsibility to willfulness should be forbidden, he writes:

> The concept of 'dehumanization' is meaningless to people who deny, as the culture increasingly does, the idea of the distinctively human. That concept seems under assault from biochemists, molecular biologists, psychiatrists and others who locate the essence of man in raw material subject to manipulation, unconstrained by any notion of a constant 'human' good.

Will goes on to conclude that "philosophy, including political philosophy, must assert sovereignty over manipulative techniques."

Will is right that many of the moral concepts of "being human" are challenged by the development of techniques of fetal implantation. But the assertion that they should be "forbidden as dehumanizing" will not do as a response. It is precisely *because* technology and the sense of the human have changed that we are confronted with the question of "wombs for rent."

Clearly what has happened here is a Foucauldian crisis point. A set of the relations that make up what we think it means to be a human person — a "man," in Foucault's terms — is under challenge by developments in what Foucault calls the "outside." In this case, it is the technology of fetal implantation and the consequent practice of "surrogate mothering." It is not hard to see even a greater challenge when recombinant DNA technology is added to this. The problem posed for us is how to think about these developments not just as a new policy problem, but as a changed notion of what it means to be a human being. This is the question of the "death of man."

Let us notice the problem that Will is having. He is faced with a very practical and important demand, that we take action, that is, that we make some sense of a particular problem, in this case "wombs for rent." With what order or framework can that problem be put in touch?

Here, again, the best move seems first to recognize that there is no good move, to refuse Will's insistence and keep silent to his question. The reasons for our dumbness are themselves instructive. It is as if we were split. On the one hand, we — political theorists — are called by the developments of the last several decades to worry about matters of monstrous import — the fate of the West, the ultimacy of ethical judgments, and so forth. For Will, this is the problem of dehumanization. On the other hand, everyday problems — abortion, the quality of work, sexuality, all call out for discussion. In the case here, this particular configuration of events led one family to seek a womb for a child they would have as theirs.

Will is quite aware that these latter problems cannot be solved on a purely ad hoc basis; he is unable to find the structure that will make convincing sense of them. More problematically, all he can do is call for an answer, on the assumption that there should be one. I will not in this book have an answer to this question. I do hope, however, to cast some light on the elements of this problem-area.[55] What kind of problem are we having here?

It is precisely not a problem that is going to be solved by the insistence on an already existing position.[56] The simple assertion of the morally and politically right will not do, if only because the "we" to which Will claims to address himself would not recognize itself in any such assertion. This is a problem to which Foucault addressed himself:

> The problem is not so much to define a political 'position' (which comes down to a choice on a pre-constituted chessboard) but to imagine and bring into existence new schemas of politicization.[57]

Despite the fact that Will calls upon political theory, he misconstrues its task. He wants it to answer the question of "wombs for rent": he wants an *answer*. Here we have a source of the difference between political theory and politics on the one hand, and theology and religion on the other. The premise of religion is that there is something that will count as an answer, even if, as with Calvin and Augustine, we are not always sure that as humans we can grasp what that answer may be. (Because of this doubt about human capacity, Calvin and Augustine have the highest appreciation of politics of any of the great theologians.) Religion tries to make us beings for whom an answer (one that exists, even if we do not see it, even if we cannot see it) counts. Political theory tries to make us beings who are able to acknowledge something as an answer.

Once we are able to allow something to count as an answer — to stand authoritatively for us — all political theory can ever do is make a particular answer obvious. This is the task of political theory: to allow us to make available to ourselves and to others a world in which something can count as an answer. It is when an answer is not obvious — not 'not obvious' in the way that it is obvious what you have to do to get to the top of Mont Blanc, but 'not obvious' in the sense that we must first know that it is a mountain that we are on — that we have a political problem, and not a religious or even an ethical one.

* * *

Such problems have had a number of different formulations over history. Take, for instance, the often maligned paragraphs that Locke devotes to "property." Locke spends considerable time in the *Second Treatise on Government* developing a theory of property which seems to rest on the right of the individual to that which he has made his own. The relation of the theory of property to the political theory that occupies the rest of the book has been much discussed. Locke has been accused (by C. B. Macpherson, among others) of fitting sheep's clothing over the raw exploitation of early capitalism; here property drives the politics, and Locke's discussion exposes his bias. Others have attempted to soften this portrait (Peter Laslett) and claim that the discussion of property is merely a stricture against greed and that far from being an early capitalist ideologue, Locke was merely a secular Calvinist, strait-laced in morals as well as in politics. Finally, Locke has also been praised (recently by Richard Ashcraft) for promoting a revolutionary theory of government; here the politics overwhelms the opinions on property. All, perhaps true, yet somehow beside my point.[58]

Locke is struck, I would say, by the difference between human beings and that which is not human beings — call it nature. Yet human beings are nothing without action, and the way in which they acquire characteristics is to interact with nature. They are concrete expressions of energy. Typically that interaction consists in the imprinting upon energy (let us call this a blank slate) of the forms of nature. So, when I pick up a plum, it becomes mine, property, still a plum, but now *my* plum, part of who I am. Yet, Locke realizes, this slate which now has one mark on it — a plum — is threatened in two manners. I am threatened — for it is "I" which is at stake — by first the fact that there was no limit to "me" — I did not know, nor did anyone else know, where I might stop. And, if I had no

limits, I also had no definition. So a first limitation was drawn
from the fact that I had to put my self to use. I could not extend myself and then let it rot away—such was contradictory
to the whole intention of the enterprise of a self: No more plums
than I could eat or barter. That no plums rotted was the sign
of a center that held. This was Locke's response to what he
saw as the threat of time.

As Locke also perceived, the self was more threatened from
another, spatial, quarter. A second guarantee was needed.
Someone might take my plums away from me, without my
consent. This would destroy the self of which those plums were
a component. Hence, the "I" required a "we" and the conditions of contract. The main task of Locke's work is the drawing of boundaries, a delineation of the self in space.

Rousseau is likewise struck by the original givenness of the
other. Rousseau's vision is more subtle and, I think, more accurate than is that of Locke. What Rousseau does is to take
some of the same concerns as had Locke and to formulate
them directly in terms of the fear of and for the self that is
their root structure. For Rousseau, there are two aspects to
our encounter with an other. Humans are endowed with very
few faculties in the state of nature; one of them is what Rousseau calls "pity." He means by this merely the capacity to recognize that another being is like oneself, rather than being
like a tree or a dog. (A sign of how important this given about
human beings is can be seen in the abortion debate: we are
struck by the fact that the fetus is human and not, say, feline.
If we were not so struck, there would be no debate.) For Rousseau, the recognition of the other takes precedence over the
recognition of the embodiment of oneself in property. (With
Locke, property had come first and had required the subsequent recognition of the other.)

Rousseau, similar to Locke but more complex, also finds
the beginning of society at the point and time at which someone finds another willing to accept the limitation of a boundary. At the beginning of the second part of *Discourse on the Origin of Inequality,* Rousseau writes that:

The first man who, having enclosed a piece of ground, to whom it occurred to say *this is mine,* found people sufficiently simple to believe him, was the true founder of civil society.

But the relationship was originally one of antagonism.

How many crimes, wars, murders, how many miseries and horrors mankind would have been spared by him who, pulling up the stakes or filling in the ditch, had cried out to his kind: Beware of listening to this impostor; you are lost if you forget that the fruits of the Earth are everyone's and the Earth is no one's.[59]

Indeed, for Rousseau, the very act of encountering an other, insofar as there actually is an encounter, is a threat. In the *Essay on the Origin of Languages,* he writes that people are brought to relation with the other not from needs, but from their passions.[60] A bit further on, in the chapter entitled "That the First Language had to be Figurative," he argues that:

A savage, upon meeting others, will at first have been frightened. His fright will have made him see these men as larger and stronger than himself; he will have called them Giants. After much experience he will have recognized that, since these supposed Giants are neither bigger nor stronger than he, their stature did not fit the idea that he initially attached to the word Giant. He will therefore invent another name common to both them and to himself, for example the name man, and he will restrict the name Giant to the false object that had struck him during his illusion.[61]

What impresses here is the way in which for Rousseau the very idea of "man" is an almost accidental resolution of an initial illusion. That we are and know ourselves as humans hangs entirely from the slender chain of experience that those whom we feared as harmful did not over time actually harm us.

Rousseau is clear about one thing: our initial experience of the other is one of fear and the naming of the other — "giant," then "man"—is the literal expression of this fear. Society can then become a way of dealing—be this in avoidance, mitigation, or in acknowledgment and transcendence—with this fear of and for the self. One need not elaborate the passages in Hegel and Marx which deal with the encountering of the other—this is the motor of the world which they set out. Society—the "we" to which appeals can be made—both is and is not a fraud. Here the self has been delineated in space, as in Locke.

Having started before Locke, Rousseau, however, goes beyond him and adds another dimension. Just as in the original state of nature there was no "we" and hence no "I", at the end of the Second Discourse, he suggests that even the spatially secured self can be threatened in time. In a series of stages, he foresees a situation in which bourgeois civilization gradually puts an end to all relations with other humans until at last man returns to a new state of nature.

> Here is the last stage of inequality, and the ultimate point which closes the circle and meets the point from which we set out: Here all private individuals again become equal, because they are nothing. . . . Here everything reverts to the sole law of the stronger and consequently to a new state of nature.[62]

I read Rousseau's text as a claim that modern civilization has made appeal to the "we" impossible.

> Civilized man . . . always active, sweats, scurries, constantly agonizes in search of still more strenuous occupations: he works to his death, even rushes towards it in order to be in a position to live. . . . The sociable man, always outside himself, only knows how to live in the opinion of others, and so to speak, derives the sentiment of his own existence solely from their judgment.[63]

I read this not just as a description of "mass society" but as a claim that the crisis of modernity may be understood not so much as deriving from the absence of the "we"—which may be true enough — but more from the unwillingness of humans to risk a "we," to find themselves in the position that they can recognize another in themselves. They live "constantly outside" of themselves. This is what is meant by a crisis of the subject.

What would this crisis consist of? It is a mistake, Nietzsche tells us, to think of nihilism as a kind of cataclysmic event in itself, even if the events of the third decade of the century and much of Nietzsche's rhetoric seem to indicate that it might be (much in the manner that Marx tended to make "the revolution" sound more apocalyptic than it need be). The more usual description is that of the prologue to *Zarathustra*, the crowd that welcomes the arrival of the last men.

What do I mean by a crisis? What seems particular to the present is that so many think of themselves as separate from others.[64] We see it in part in the relentless pursuit of community — Fraternity, Thoreau wrote, is a word on everyone's lips and in no one's heart.

That this has been a central problem in the West for a long time is apparent when we look at the central problems to which our philosophy has addressed itself from at least the time of Descartes and Machiavelli. It is no accident that it is on the problem of the "we" and its lack, the problem of the other, that our philosophy has chosen to dwell. Descartes's demon deceiver is well known. Machiavelli saw in relations to other precisely the source of lack of control on the part of the prince. One was best off if one owed nothing to fortune but opportunity and was able to change one's shape at will.[65] Hobbes felt obliged to begin the *Leviathan* with a demonstration that we are not dreaming. Richard Rorty, in a well-known recent book,[66] has traced out the vicissitudes of the epistemological turn that accompanies the need to ground our understanding of the world on self-certainty of vision. He assumes that we do not need such philosophy and can simply stop doing it. What is not clear in his book is why he thinks that we can get rid of the philosophy and not the world to which the philosophy was handmaiden. Were we to do this, we should at least have to begin to accept that to know another we need not have his or her thoughts and feelings.

One of the solutions offered by Western thought to the problem of the unavailability of the other has been what I might call the theatricalization of the self, the transformation of the self into a set of roles and set behaviors. Machiavelli is the Stanislavsky of politics and *The Prince* is an actor's handbook. Hobbes sought to build an artificial being, who would have in human affairs the perfection he would still admit that God had put into the natural world. This will be the subject of the second chapter.

Second, a sign of the times is the demand or the expectation that we somehow develop a "science" of human knowledge. Stanley Cavell points out that the demand for a science of human behavior means that we do not know ourselves, that we feel this as a lack, and that we have some expectations that we should and can get that knowledge.[67] The question is whether or not our insistence on science becomes a way to avoid acknowledging ourselves. This will be the subject of the third chapter.

Third, we do not find our life in our thought. In political theory, this means that we do not find ourselves in our texts. This would mean that we are unable to find the problems which move us in our texts. There are two reasons for this. The first is that we may know ourselves insufficiently well to recognize ourselves in the texts. In the readings of Locke and Rousseau I gave above, I was trying to suggest that there was, in fact, no reason to throw out the tradition of political theory—in the manner in which, say, John Gunnell has recently urged us.[68] But these are but fragmentary beginnings of a rereading responsive to our times. The other reason would be that we would have a new set of experiences to deal with—I alluded to some possibilities. In that case we have no real words for them.

Here some direction may come from the groping towards a philosophy in which the body—I mean the incarnate fleshliness or our being-in-the-world—plays an important role. Here there may be the beginnings of a rejection of a philosophy in which the mental was seen as the source of incorrigibility. Such a beginning takes many forms. As noted above, it is in great part thrust upon us by external developments. Economics have driven women into the marketplace and all that seemed solid in that field has, in Marx's terms, melted into thin air. The debate that rages around abortion seems clearly to admit only ad hoc solutions for liberals. One hundred and forty years ago, in the eleventh thesis on Feuerbach, "All previous philosophy has merely interpreted the world, the problem, however, is to change it", Marx came to the realization that human activity was philosophically significant, not just as a subject for, but as a component of philosophy. Feminist thought is forcing us (who is the "we" here?) to a new, possibly transformed Thomism in which we take biological differences as philosophically serious. These matters will be the subject of the fourth chapter.

What should we retain from this initial discussion? Five things:

First, that politics is that form of human activity in which the answer to the question "who am I?" is also the answer to the question "who are we?"

Second, that this answer is related to, but importantly different from the answers given by ethics, religion, and so forth.

Third, that authority and community are completely intertwined questions.

Fourth, that the exploration of the authority of the "we" shows a crisis in the notion of the subject, of the person—a crisis of our time.

Fifth, that this crisis has to do with the coming to ground in political theory of a broader concern of Western philosophy and life—the problem of the other.

We lack what political theory has always given us, a text. I shall return to the question of text and community in the last chapter. Let me note here that the fear of the growing ineffectiveness of a shared text of politics is at least as old and as age-bound as Thucydides' comments in *The Peloponnesian*

War and as recent as Orwell's elaboration of Newspeak. One might ask oneself in closing what forms of writing might in a transitional age best raise the possibility of a community of discourse. I draw here upon Nietzsche and Wittgenstein.

First is silence. I mean: not saying anything. This will perhaps prove controversial, or at least unsatisfactory, for we theorists are often as naturally garrulous as politicians. Yet if the changes in the world of persons and the political world are of the magnitude and scope that they sometimes appear to be, there are many situations in which we will not only not know precisely what to say, but *where anything we say will necessarily be wrong*. The forcefulness of the plays of Samuel Beckett derives from their ability to evoke this awareness of our condition: that now in politics, as perhaps for many in the past in religion, and perhaps as Nietzsche argued in the future in morality, men and women wait in an endgame, unable to stop yet unsure of why they are going on. We have all encountered miniature versions — perhaps all versions are in *pianissimo* — in our personal life and we know the difficulty we have in shutting up.[69] It is, I would contend, a first step towards our own condition to recognize that at times there may simply be nothing to say. (Why, Beckett was asked, with your despair about language, do you continue to write? — That is what I am trying to find out.)

Perhaps this is not much of a contribution. Silence is not the last word, indeed, not even the first. But it is a recognition like the one we saw in Weber's vocation addresses that there are times when anything we say will be *parti pris,* ideological, hopelessly one-sided. Government itself, at these times, as Hegel noted in the chapter on "Absolute Freedom and Terror" in the *Phenomenology,* can only "exhibit itself . . . as a faction."

Second, there are other forms of writing now somewhat in vogue in certain philosophical quarters that may provoke rather than instruct, call forth a "we" in a recontextualized community of readers. I am thinking here of the experimentation going on in France or Richard Rorty's calls for "edifying discourse." I do this without beating a drum for Derrida,

Deleuze, Guattari, or even Foucault and their usage of the gnomic and aphoristic, the playful and the misleading. But these forms are worth taking seriously, even if that be a *contradictio in adverbo*.

The aphorism is a prototype for the way of understanding writing to which I am referring. At first encounter it may appear meaningful, superficial, trivially true, or simply nonsense. The writing thus provokes an automatic selectivity of interest: only those who find themselves in it will continue to listen. Others, who do not react, will not react. In an important sense, the provocation was not meant for them — they are not part of this community. In this sense, the aphorism is the pure fool, the Parsifal of discourse. The attempt to uncover and discover its nature and name will stir up the fermentation that rests within it, much in the way that Oedipus brings himself to light.

The aphoristic approach — reading as if the text were an aphorism — admits of categorical thought only with difficulty. Indeed, it is the discovery of the categories of the context and structure in which the statement makes sense which is the question. A serious reader of an aphorism is forced to participate in the creation of a common world, which, if successful, may penetrate below the point of simple acquiescence until a world is available that appears as perfectly and transparently true.

Another form of discourse which creates a community of discourse, a "we," is the riddle. This seems to be the preferred form in philosophy when nothing other than perfect clarity will do. In a riddle, the reader is given a set of seemingly unrelated elements ("black and white and red all over") and asked to come up with a constitutive logic for this landscape. When the seeker has arrived at an answer, the problem disappears — such was the traditional fate of the Sphinx. It is literally impossible to pose a riddle twice, so much so that we tend to avoid putting ourselves in the position of asking a riddle of someone already informed, "Stop me if you have heard this one".

Riddles are possible forms of inquiry and discourse appropriate to situations in which one does not know one's way about with the material at hand—when, in other words, the problems are of a philosophical and theoretical nature. The apparently innocent beginning of the first chapter of Rousseau's *Social Contract*—"Man is born free and is everywhere in chains. How did he arrive in this state? I don't know. What can render it legitimate? That is the intention of this work"—expresses Rousseau's intention to bind together morally those elements of the social world, the anthropological dissociation of the existence of which he had shown in the *Second Discourse.* There he had demonstrated the derivation of the gulf separating man and citizen; in the *Social Contract,* he attempts to make sense of those facts of contemporary society that appear to him as a riddle: "How is it that man is born free and is everywhere in chains?" The task is not to explain—"That I do not know"—but to make whole.

Read in this manner, the *Social Contract* becomes not Rousseau's idea of what would be a good state, but the description of the "we" that can seriously be meant when we speak of a good state. It is an articulation of a landscape—I should say a city—in which the "we" is made available to its members. In this it is different from the city described in the first social contract of the *Second Discourse,* a social contract that resolved the spatial definition of a person, but not the members' temporal dissolution.

A riddle is then only a riddle when someone makes it one. It is a formulation of states of affairs, a form of discourse in which all data are given. The problem is not to discover some new element, which will bring all of the other ones into coherence, but to figure out a way to see already existent data in such a way that they make sense together. We will return to this theme in chapter three. All that we need to know is there to be known; the answer will make clear what is going on, so much so that one may feel mildly upset at "not getting it at first sight." Lévi-Strauss's analysis unwittingly brings out the political theoretical aspect of riddling. He writes that the riddle "brings together elements doomed to remain separate. . . . The answer succeeds, against all expectations, in getting back to its question."[70]

Such discourse would be inherently political in form when politics no longer knows its way about. It would remind us of the necessary and permanent disjuncture, linkage, and tension between the claim of the individual, outrageous though it seem in riddle and aphorism, and the particular social arrangement which might result from such a claim. Additionally, and perhaps more importantly, although work done in such a vein may sometimes appear foolish and foolery, if done well it can attest to what remains the ultimate hope, that men and women be serious and responsible enough to themselves and each other to realize that their work will be witness to their words.

2. THE PROMISE AND LURE OF AESTHETICS: POLITICAL THEORY AND THE RECOGNITION OF PERSONS

> Now at this century's impressive close
> As actuality itself is turned
> To art and we see mighty natures locked
> In Struggle for a goal of lofty import, . . .
> > now,
> Art is allowed assay of higher flight
> Upon its shadow stage; indeed, it must be
> Lest it be put to shame by life's own stage.
> > Friedrich Schiller, "Prologue"
> > *Wallenstein's Camp*

> Eyes seeking the response of eyes
> Bring out the stars, bring out the flowers,
> Thus concentrating earth and skies
> So none need be afraid of size.
> All revelation has been ours.
> > Robert Frost, *All Revelation*

I

IN THE first chapter, I raised the question of the status of the "we," the appeal to which was the basis of what we mean by politics. I suggested that it was the role of political theory to make a text available such that we could find the "I" and the "we" in or as part of it. The recognition of others was thus seen as a fundamental aspect of the political and making the acknowledgment of the other an unavoidable experience was the role of political theory.

With this we approach the tense relationship of theory to drama, the realm in which recognition of self and other has always played a central role. But what is the source of the age-old hostility of political theory to drama? We have all read Plato's apparent excoriation of the poets;[1] we know that Rousseau's civic sense prompted him to address a lengthy letter in rebuke to the cosmopolitan d'Alembert for his proposal to establish a theater in Geneva in order to join in that city "the wisdom of Laecedemonia to the grace of Athens";[2] we remember that the advent of Puritanism marked difficult times for an English theater that had recently seen the achievements of Shakespeare.[3] Yet, on first reflection, this should appear a bit strange: Does not theater address many of the same issues and teach many of the same lessons as political theory? Are not the great dramas, as critics from Aristotle to Hegel have recognized, dramas about the problems of integrating societies faced with the demands of moral and social change? Plato was surely close enough to Aeschylus to have understood what his contemporary Aristophanes was making clear in *The Frogs,* that this playwright was above all concerned with the civic virtue of the polis. Jean-Pierre Vernant, for instance, has argued persuasively that "the true subject matter of tragedy is the social thought which is particular to that individual city" and that in fact "tragedy is born only when one begins to look upon myth with the eye of a citizen."[4] One might think then that political theorists would have enlisted the service of dramatists to further them in their aims. Instead one finds that most of the critics of theater require the elimination of the institution of theater itself, and not simply proper censorship of the subject matter.[5] Somehow, what theater is and does constitutes a problem, a problem which is not in principle solved by controls.[6]

Whatever hostility may have existed in the past, it seems to be changing. As late as 1870, an actor could be denied a Christian burial in New York City. For most of the 1980s, the

United States had a president who based his popularity pre-cisely on that which in years gone by would have disqualified him.[7]

As a form of human activity and of discourse theater seems to have both a bond and a distance from political theory. By exploring the ambivalence of that relationship, by reopening the question of the differences and antagonisms between po-litical theory and theater, one can find out what it means to participate in each community of discourse. I propose to show in this chapter that this is a central truth to the critique that Rousseau and Plato and the others launched against theater. There is an antagonism, but the antagonism is to our benefit. We will learn, I hope to show, something about ourselves both as political persons and as actors. One is not forced to choose between them, if only one keeps the requirements of change in mind.

Aristotle points out in the *Poetics* that tragedy is the *mimesis* of *praxis* or action.[8] He means by this that tragic drama is not concerned to portray characters, but rather "life" in its happi-ness and misery. The characters are there — the play needs them — so that this portrayal may have form, but it is, he in-sists, the action that is our focus. We are not concerned with Oedipus' qualities, but with what he *does*. Here is a profound understanding, not fully developed in Aristotle's text. For in saying that drama is the *mimesis* of action, Aristotle was on the verge of distinguishing theater from all other art forms (with the possible exception of music, to which, as we know from Nietzsche and others, it bears a profound relationship). More specifically, in saying that theater is the "imitation of action," Aristotle was implying that in the theater we, in the audience, do not experience the distancing from the aesthetic object that is found in other art forms. Theater is not the pre-sentation of an object which is other than the artwork. What we have before us is something that the artist cannot directly face (as in the case with painting and sculpture[9]), nor that is spatially defined as an art-object (e.g., a book). Rather we are presented with actual bodies, beings that definably resemble ourselves, and which are not, as Michael Goldman has noted,[10] their products. There is no distinction between what the "actors-as-characters" are doing and the play as we-as-spectators encounter it. What I might call the "wrought" quality of a play is not present to us in the same objectified fashion as is a painting, a sculpture, or even a movie.[11] In these other forms, the objecthood of the artifact reminds us of the artist;[12] not so in drama.

It is in the very presentness of the stage (when we are members of the audience) that we find the strong parallel to our lives as we live them "ordinarily." In our ordinary lives we do not feel that we are the result of someone else's direction or creative act. It is worth noting that "ordinary" lives are not necessarily the ones that we live as a matter of course. If our life is religious, a case that for many was and is a matter of course, we know that it is God that "has made us and not we ourselves."[13]

Both in the theater and in our lives we encounter corporeality, bodies; what we encounter we do not encounter as object.[14] Indeed, our very notions of personhood and identity are dependent upon the feeling that our self is autonomous. Here there is a clue to a common theme in theater and political theory: both are concerned with the process whereby an individual comes to encounter him- or herself as who he or she is—as a human being. We are concerned then with identity, personhood, how a life is led.[15]

Theater, as we saw with Aristotle, and life, as we now see, can be understood in terms of this activity. To live a life in the world as persons, we must make the understandings of the world which serve to form and identify who we are available to our self. This cannot be done without those understandings being available to others. Any number of understandings are possible: we will not speak of identity unless a certain coherence is achieved. Who we are, I might then say, is a question of coherence, of construction and the assimilation of particular worldviews. The question will be the kind and degree of coherence.

The Distance between Theater and Ordinary Life

The above tries to establish the closeness of theater and ordinary life. But we do — most of the time — know that our life
is not theater, or at least that the theater is somewhere we visit,
somewhere different. When Jacques proclaims in a moment
of bitter self-consciousness in *As You Like It* that everything
about the world is stage, and the men and women but bit players who enter with birth and exit with death, he is making
an important and instructive mistake. Jacques says that the
whole world is theater and only theater, that there is nothing
else. This speech leads in the next scene to his departure from
the Ardennes woods. Shakespeare seems to be indicating that
anyone who seriously thinks as does Jacques about the world
cannot live with others, cannot participate even in the blithe
erotic politics of identity that occupy Rosalind and the others.
Jacques thus does not recognize that for the self to be able
to live with others, all the world cannot be a stage, that our
knowledge of the world cannot be complete and completed.

What would it mean not to be a person, not to live with
others? It could mean to be a king, or a god, an animal, or
perhaps a philosopher. Aristotle remarks that neither gods
nor beasts need to live with others. But what kind of being
is a god; what is it actually like to live alone? It was the
achievement of Kant's critical thought, and the most important move in moral philosophy since Socrates, to show that
human beings are limited in their faculties and that these limits are not a fault in our ability to deal with the world and
others, but are rather the very condition of our being able to
do so. Jacques, we might say, shows us that no one who thinks
that the whole world is a stage can live *with* others. Is it then
in the nature of the stage that the bodies who live on it[16] are
without limits?[17]

Being as a god, without limits, has been a temptation in
the West, at least since humans sought morality and domination over nature. Calvin, for instance, saw the temptations of
divinity very strongly and, in a vein that anticipates Kant by

almost two hundred and fifty years, argued against them in the name of the city:

> Therefore when it is asked "why did God do thusly?" one must answer, because He willed it [*Il l'a voulu*]. And if one goes further and asks, 'Why did He will it?' one asks for something greater and higher than the will of God. Thus let human temerity control itself and not seek that which is not, for fear of not finding that which is. . . . For of those things which it is neither lawful nor possible to know, ignorance is learning [*en est docte*]; the desire to know them is a species of fury [*rage*].[18]

If Calvin's perspective, and Kant's, are at all accurate, then the central human sin, that which keeps us from being ourselves, is the temptation to become a being without limits. Hubris, pride, these are and must be a denial of the self, of what it is possible to be at any given time.

Politics, we might say, is the particularly human enterprise. In Plato's *Protagoras,* for instance, we are proposed a myth whereby humans are given politics as the remedy for their lack of the natural qualities which would otherwise have ensured their survival. And in that sense politics is the activity whereby humans have given themselves a particular identity, and separated themselves as members of a group different from all other groups. Political theory has been the recognition and formulation of that identity. If this be true, then we may begin to see part of the profound ambiguity that political thinkers have always reserved for the stage. Solon fled in despair from one of the early theatrical representations in Athens. When Thespis argued to him that it was after all not real and only a game, he is purported to have responded that it would not be long until one saw the effects of such games on the relations of citizens.[19] His perception was profound and wise — it is essentially that of Rousseau. But he fails, as did Rousseau, to explore the nature of the tension and to see that the desire to abrogate the tension will in fact diminish the vitality of the world of politics.

The most important thing about theater seems to lie precisely in the fact that the characters on stage do, in some way, escape the limits of being human. While they are not gods, they are heroic beings, above the ordinary human run. As Michael Goldman notes: "While on stage, the actors enjoy a kind of omnipotence, a privilege and protection not unlike that accorded sacred beings."[20] Aristotle himself, in the *Problemata,* had already drawn attention to the fact that the heroes in tragedy were less "human" than the chorus, marking by that note that neither were, really.[21] Humans, as opposed to actors-as-characters, live their lives, and to be lived those lives must, all of them, come into being and to an end. Actors-as-characters are, on the other hand, in Goldman's words again, "phenomenologically immortal." They do not live, and this is precisely their importance to us. Were Cordelia a person outside the stage, we would have to be concerned with her as a person. On stage it is her action which commands our attention and we pay attention to the world that is created by what she and the others do. To the extent that the play is successful, it provides its own terms of reference. We do not judge action by whether or not it is "real" but rather by the terms of the world in which we, like Claudius, have been caught. The play *is* the thing.

Why? It is an achievement, perhaps in the end the only lasting one, of the "new criticism" to focus our attention on the work of art and not to worry, as L. C. Knights once delightfully put it, about "how many children Lady Macbeth had." In this the New Critics perhaps shared the philosophical positivism which immediately preceded and surrounded them. But they did, as did the positivists, focus on the work itself, on what was *given,* and thus on a whole. In doing so they allowed readers (whom they conceived of as ideal critics rather than as an audience for literature) to turn away from the inexhaustibility of the everday world.[22] Their move was salutary even if it took later critics to help us see that a work of art was more complex than they had thought.[23]

Drama, then, gives us an experience unique in the arts (again with the possible exception of music). It gives us a world which, if sufficiently well-wrought, is whole and complete, without the burred and ragged edges that our historical days must have. That is, I think, the true meaning of Aristotle's reference in the *Poetics* to an "action complete in itself . . . [with a] beginning . . . which is not itself necessarily after anything else and which has something naturally after itself; an end . . . with nothing else after it."[24] The point to Aristotle's discussion of the unities is that in theater there can be nothing outside of what happens, which is precisely not the case in a part of our lives. It is the very completeness and perfection of the stage that makes it special.

Consider for a moment the difference between theater and film. In film, even in black and white film, we have necessarily the sense of a world screened and reproduced for us. The mechanical elements in film, especially its automatic quality, keep the world which is on the screen from being present to us. A film is a reflection, literally and ontologically. Thus, no matter what the pretensions of cinema — Eisenstein is perhaps the most important offender — there is a world beyond that with which we are inevitably presented. The medium itself calls attention to that which is screened, in both senses. Reflect, for instance, that in cinema but not in theater we wonder about the "star" — a person with an off-stage existence, real or putative. In theater, the action given to us by the actors as they are characters calls to mind nothing but itself.[25]

Is the Stage Just a Stage?

I recognize that this is highly contentious. Let me take two obvious counterexamples: the so-called "alienation-effect" of Bertolt Brecht, and audience participation theater such as was current about fifteen years ago with the Living Theater or in some of the early work of Richard Schechner.

Brecht tries — sometimes more in theory than in practice — to preserve the political message in his plays by constantly reminding the audience that they are "watching a play." This is necessary so that the audience member can preserve his or her critical faculty and resist being swept up on stage. Brecht's concerns are thus much like those that Rousseau had in the *Lettre à d'Alembert*.[26] Rousseau thought that the danger of the theater was that it gave people emotions in an irresponsible and motile fashion. He argued that being a spectator meant abandoning responsibility for one's emotions; furthermore, since the world of the stage was artificial, the emotions of the spectators had no necessary and natural object and were thus apt to be misused elsewhere.[27] Likewise, Brecht wants to keep spectators from forgetting their faculties of critical rationality. Only thus will the lesson learned in the theater be secured for the world outside. I cannot argue here about the possibility of this understanding and whether or not Brecht actually ever achieves it.[28] It is important to note that Brecht is trying to save the audience from the fate to which Rousseau thought it was doomed. Brecht's vision retains the understanding that the stage is an ambiguous form of existence. It is the audience member who, by the alienation-effect, is to be kept from corruption.[29]

The development of "audience participation" theater by the Living Theater and other groups in the late 1960s is something entirely different. I would argue that although their intention is to give us (those going to the theater) an authentic (unstaged) experience by breaking down the boundaries between the audience and the stage, they leave us not with an authentic emotion, but in confusion. We know not who we are, nor who these people coming at us are, nor why we should pay attention to them. This is neither theater — there are no characters — nor politics — there are no persons, only a crowd and sometimes a mob.[30]

I have claimed that the theater gives us a *whole* world, complete to itself, which does not call along with it a world other than itself. As such, I am then suggesting that drama performs — can perform — for life a function analogous to, but even beyond that which Kant sought to do in the *Critiques*. The knowledge he hoped to gain in those writings was not knowledge of matters of fact; indeed, he demonstrated that were we to remain with only knowledge of facts, the only possible intellectual position would be solipsism. Instead, he shows us knowledge of what we must be or accept about ourselves before or when we seek knowledge of the facts of this world. As Stanley Cavell puts it, such answers as Kant gives are "meant to provide us [not with] more knowledge of facts, but with [the knowledge of] what would count as various 'matters of fact'."[31] Kant, then, shows us what we will be doing when we are doing anything in particular; drama goes beyond this, we might say, and shows us something DONE, both in the sense of something accomplished and in the sense of being performed.

It is this fact that stands as the center of what I am calling the perfectedness of the stage. Though in ordinary life we might worry or at least think about what circumstances are connected to the life of those we meet, on stage these characters are for and in themselves only. In both *King Lear* and *The Tempest* we are confronted with a man trying to continue his presence in the world through the activity of his daughter. In terms of the play, we never think of or, more precisely, we never entertain seriously the question of mother and daughter. My point, of course, is not that Shakespeare reveals an anti-maternal bias, but that the play is such that this question cannot seriously concern us. Miranda is assured that her mother was "a piece of virtue" and for her, as for the audience, this is sufficient for that present. The world of a play, as a piece of music, closes in on itself in a creative repetition and lives only in its own present, with neither past nor future. Lear dies, Prospero bids farewell (to whom?) and what lives after is no longer the character, nor, of course, the actor, but US, the audience. This understanding has perhaps nowhere been dramatically so advanced as in Peter Handke's *Offending the Audience,* which consists of four actors on stage enforcing on the audience that they, out there, are *the* theatrical event. Like a Brecht play inside out, Handke asserts only part of the theatrical experience, but the exercise is an effective reminder.

The New Critics were struck by the fact that there was no

world outside the text: thus we need not worry about Miranda's mother. I am struck by the fact that we experience a whole
world in the text, a world of which Miranda's mother is not
a part. The action of the stage shows us what something *is;*
in somewhat exalted language, it is, or can be, the realm of
being. And it is here that we catch a further insight into the
hostility of Plato, Rousseau, and all those who emphasize the
dangers of theater. Drama possesses the awful finality of perfection, not in the moral sense, but in the sense that no change
can be made in it without making it something other than
it is. The world in which we live ordinarily is multiple and
inexhaustible, always more than we can make of it. Things
are never finally what they are, for they suffer change and
transformation. But these problems and perplexities, in which
political theorists from Plato to Nietzsche have taught us to
see ourselves, do not pertain to those beings on stage. Perhaps
they resemble us, but they are possessed of a divine state[32]
such that they are perfect in what they do and without limitations for how we view them. It is not then surprising that many
writers have thought drama to be immoral: it is very close to
looking upon the gods themselves, and to claim to see God
has always been either blasphemous or separate from the ordinary human realm.

If we want to see what making love means, we can do no
better than to watch *A Midsummer's Night Dream;* if we want to
know the terrors and the life of talking with one another, we
will learn it best from *Endgame.* I have now moved to "ontological thought" in my assertion that drama can show us the true
meaning of particular activities which we engage in — and par-
enthetically that politics cannot and should not. Drama can
do this because it is not subject to the inexhaustibility of actual life and is therefore free to show us the reality of a particular action. Naturally, that is, ordinarily, it is silly and pre-
posterous, immoral in fact, for Creon to wall up Haemon and
Antigone, much as it is for the chorus not to rush to their aid.
But that is what makes it a play. The act alone convinces and
provides us the terms by which we understand it.[33] Of course,

Lear is a fool to avoid Cordelia's words and she a twit to insist on them. But concern with such crotchety senility is not important: it is his inability to acknowledge his daughter rather than the fact that she can require him to do so which concerns us.[34] Understanding drama by reference to mental states is as reductionist as it would be by relevance to the class position of the author. (I should note that it is not irrelevant, but it is, if one stays with this only, reductionist.[35]) Drama — indeed, most art — has this for its audience: it makes available a world about which all questions can be answered and in which we see the perfection of our reasons and understanding. We should not confuse such a world with that of ordinary life, even though we may be tempted to do so. For that world does not appear as other and alien, but merely as perfect, and perfection has its attractions.

II

I have been speaking in increasingly general terms. It is time now to bring the understanding of drama which I have been proposing together with the practice of political theory in order to see what tensions exist in fact between them and with what light they illuminate each other. I have indicated that political theory is concerned with the acts by which humans mutually define their lives with others who are not their immediate blood relations. As such the polis is the first political form, certainly in the West and probably in the world. The polis marks the move away from a magical conception of the world in which humans are not differentiated from nature, as well as from the blood relations of the tribe and the *oikos,* and most importantly away from notions of self that are dependent on custom or simple preeminence. The polis corresponds to that time when individuals come to a more or less autonomous sense of themselves such that they require of themselves that they interact with others on terms of their mutual choosing.[36]

The matter is complex, for, from Aristotle on, this mutuality has also been recognized as one of the central characteristics of tragedy, if not of all drama.[37] In the *Poetics,* during his discussion of the finest form of complex tragedy, Aristotle points to a central occurrence which he sees in the best of tragedies. He calls it *anagnorisis,* the change from "ignorance to knowledge . . . in the characters marked for good or evil fortune."[38] *Anagnorisis* means to recognize, to come to know, to reveal oneself. It is used only in the context of persons and leads to a change in the understanding of self and others. Most important is the fact that Aristotle chooses for his description of the central moments of tragedy a term which is directly linked to the question of persons, of one person to another, of one person to him- or herself. Coming to be seen and to see another is apparently for Aristotle the defining and central moment of drama.

Much of Greek tragedy may in fact be understood as built around the problems of *anagnorisis.* Aristotle has in mind here most specifically the *Oedipus Tyrannos* (which tends to serve him as the exemplar for all tragedy)[39] and specifically of that moment in which Oedipus, in relentless pursuit of the person identified with the coming of the plague afflicting Thebes, has pushed the messenger to reveal facts which must convince him (Oedipus) of what in fact his own life has signified, of who he is. Oedipus had taken himself for certain: his fault is that he was too sure of who he is, too sure that Apollo was speaking of Merope and Polybus when queried as to his true parents. He has left the question of the Sphinx too general, as it were, and assumed that "man" was a sufficient answer to who is "*dipous, tripous, tetrapous.*" Now he finds that questions about humans require specific answers; he must find out who is *Oidipous.* Thus as Oedipus comes to see himself, his recognition focuses on his identity, not only his motives or his autonomous responsibility. He consists simply of the reality that he is the being who has committed these particular acts.[40]

Oedipus discovers himself. Our shock and horror as the audience cannot be simply the discovery of the fact that he has found out that he murdered his father and is the incestuous consort of his mother. After all, we knew this already, and, as Jocasta says, "all men do these things in their dreams." What has happened is more complex. Oedipus has finally achieved for himself that identity that we in the audience knew all along to be his. His self-recognition has achieved a perfection: he stands before us as complete as he can be, revealed once and for all that he is and will be and has been. The audience thus finds corporeally before it what it had until then only known to be true. It is now in the presence of perfection. There is terror in the knowledge that there is nothing else to know and that all revelation is now ours. Nietzsche knew this well enough to make it the central motif of the approach of eternal return in his parable of the *Gay Science.* It is the demon who comes to announce that all that happens has happened already.[41] In the *Colonnus,* Oedipus will also come to see and accept this demon as the accomplishment of his life. Then he will find that whereas blasphemy had once made him into the scapegoat of Thebes, now it will qualify him as the divine king of Athens.[42]

III

I have the sense that what I have claimed above is the hardest part of what I want to argue. I repeat it once more, to emphasize it and perhaps to make it clearer. Central to the horror and exultation of tragedy is the fact that at a central moment "it is accomplished." This moment consists in what Aristotle has called the "recognition of persons": it is that moment in which there is transparency of vision, in which all is clear. At that time, the actor-as-character assumes for us a role something like what we would feel were we to encounter a ghost: it is there, complete, unavoidable, with an immortal and unchanging self. As Michael Goldman has noted, the anagnoretical character can neither be avoided nor accepted. For "we can't hit back at any ghost any more than we can ignore him . . ." because he is "so untouchable that he seems to be inside us."[43]

How do such scenes work? What is their significance for those of us interested in the relation between politics and drama? We are given an indication of the deep problem that lies here in the fact that such moments of recognition take place in speech and acknowledgment. It cannot be the acquisition of more knowledge that is the important part of the effect produced in the audience — that we know "how it comes out" seems secondary for us, and certainly was for the Greeks for whom the plot was ancestrally known.[44] Everything we need to know, we know, yet there is something particular in the revelation which gives this knowledge its awe-ful and potentially joyful character. It is to the *act* of saying that one is, that one should look to see the difference that reveals and completes the character.

Let me take another example and try to work back to this more difficult case. Suppose that you have in some manner harmed me and are sorry for it. Say that it was an oversight on your part. You are sorry, I know that you are sorry, and you know that I know that you are sorry. But the reconciliation cannot be effected until you actually *say* "I am sorry."[45] Knowing is not enough; nor is this simply what we have learned to call a performative: it is the *acknowledgment of the performance* of the action by the other that gives it actuality. You have to show me: the only way in this case is to say it. Then there is a "we."

The problem here is to understand the differences between how characters are revealed to an audience and how persons reveal themselves to each other. In theater, characters are revealed to themselves and to each other on stage. The importance of this, however, is how the effect of recognition is produced in the audience. What is its nature? What difference does it make to us, members of an audience, to have those characters on stage say those things in each other's presence? It is not quite the same as if *you* said "I am sorry" to *me,* yet there does not appear to be a complete difference of kind either.

Being an audience member has always been recognized as a form of behavior that has close links to the political. The great festivals in Athens and elsewhere in Greece were among other things a reaffirmation of those principles and victories that made Athens what it was. They were an assertion of the particular character — one might say of the self of the community. What is celebrated in the Oedipus plays, for instance, or in any of Shakespeare's plays, is the particular community, a "we" — with its laws, customs, and practices as revealed, deconstructed, and regained.

It is clear that the act of being an audience member involves changes in what is seen as acceptable behavior. We have all heard the story of the racist bumpkin running up on stage at the end of *Othello*. His behavior is wrong because he has not recognized that, for the time being at least, that which transpires on stage admits of criteria different from those that define ordinary, nontheatrical life. It is also clear that the stage treats of matters that are the very stuff of ordinary life and politics. What then is the difference? The first and most obvious answer has to do with the fact that what takes place on the stage is "pretense"; the limits of what can actually be put on the stage are the limits of that which can be pretended.

That said, the relation is still tricky. J. L. Austin once pointed out that when one goes too far in pretending (say that while you are pretending to be a hyena you take a bite out of my leg), one has not made the illusion real (you have not become a hyena) but rather one has shattered the whole world involved.[46] This also holds true for the theater. While perhaps I can love you and pretend to do so, I cannot both pretend to kill you and actually do so (although, as in *Pagliacci,* I can pretend to pretend to). Theatricality seems to me dependent on the fact that the perfection achieved by the stage requires that the actions pretended not be part of the everyday life of the person playing the character. I can pretend to love you, and can actually do so, but unless I keep the theater and ordinary life distinct, the acting-action will suffer.[47] Jean-Louis Barrault once remarked that while on stage actors lived only in the present and meant by this that they should not be conscious of (*"really* have") the emotions they were portraying.[48] The reason (or one of them) that theater is not religion is that the performance cannot require that I kill someone, nor give birth, nor die, without breaking the perfection of the theater and spilling the action over into our lives. The drama would no longer work for the action would not be complete in itself. This is why it is probably inappropriate to call gladiator spectacles or circuses true theater. This may even hold true for fornication on stage as per stage directions (*Oh! Calcutta*).[49]

It is precisely this importance of pretense in theater that stands at the bottom of Rousseau's objections, as it did at those of Solon. Rousseau's criticism here is probably the most important part of his (self-admittedly) sometimes confused essay. He argues that in the theater we (as audience) may have "pure" emotions, but that this is because they (the emotions) do not affect us; in some sense they are not really ours. Thus one can afford to be upset, for in the theater "nothing is required" from a spectator. By "nothing is required" Rousseau means that our emotions have no life-consequences; it is, as it were, irresponsible to be an audience member, as if one were on holiday from the daily and ordinary life of a citizen. To this objection, I can now respond in a preliminary manner (to be developed below) that what Rousseau has not understood is that the experience of being a member of an audience might allow one the space needed to sort out the various elements of one's identity while making a resolution. It is ironic that Rousseau, the man who almost single-handedly inaugurated the modern notion of a person as divided against him- or herself by an immoral world, should have thought that the experience of being an audience member was one of isolation. That said, his understanding remains important, for he understood that the theater was neither harmless nor without effect.

I have said that the theater is a full and self-contained world. Most important to its analysis seems to be the realization that some texts are best analyzed, as Stanley Fish has persuasively argued, not in terms of what the text *means,* but in terms of what it *does.* Indeed, the search for the meaning of a drama may be a generally misguided enterprise, or at least a diversion. Perhaps, Fish remarks, "the word 'meaning' should be discarded since it carries with it the notion of message or point. The meaning of an utterance . . . is its experience — all of it — and that experience is immediately compromised the moment you try and say anything about it."[50]

To be an audience means to be transformed, not simply to sit passively and be taken in. I shall now attempt an extended analysis of this process and try to make some sense of the relation between stage and audience. The theater provides a good entry into our problem because as an audience member one may acknowledge the force and feel the effect of the stage without having to worry about ordinary reality or the "truth" of events.

Nietzsche's analysis in the *Birth of Tragedy* of the bridge and separation between the audience and the stage is, I think, among the most incisive. I do not intend to deal with all the problematic aspects of the historical validity of his opinions on Euripides or the origin of the chorus. What matters is his analysis of how tragedy produced its effect, an analysis which he sought for some time to make concrete in Germany through the music-dramas of Richard Wagner. Characteristically, Nietzsche places great emphasis on the physical relation of the audience and the stage in a Greek theater. The setting and perspective are the necessary preliminaries for the transformation sought. In *Birth of Tragedy* he writes:

> A public of spectators as we know it was unknown to the Greeks: in their theaters, the terraced structure of the concentric arcs of the spectator-place made it possible for everyone actually to *overlook* the whole world of culture around him and to imagine in sated contemplation that he was a chorist.[51]

The German word for "overlook" is *übersehen.* Both languages permit the same double meaning of "survey" and "fail to see."

I read this passage as a whole to mean that the audience lacks nothing for its experience (it is in "sated contemplation") during the time that it is in the particular location of the "spectator-place." It has before it *only that* which is on stage, a complete world. The intensity of the focus is such that other worlds (those of culture, of everyday life) could at the same time be taken account of, ignored, and subsumed onto the stage.[52]

As spectators, the audience knows that there is nothing that it can do about anything which occurs on stage. Indeed, this is what makes it an audience member, as opposed to a well-meaning rustic. Everything that occurs on stage has an awesome necessity to it and there is nothing that anyone can do about the drama unrolling before their eyes, even though they know what is going to happen. The spectator will not, as Nietzsche continues, "run up on stage and free the God from his torments."

On stage, in addition to the various protagonists (the characters), there is the chorus, originally of dionysian and satyr ancestry, according to Nietzsche. What is important is that the chorus does not participate in the action of the protagonists. It gives advice, bewails, warns, praises, but it does not take part in the action.[53] In the fact that it does not act, it is much like the spectators who also do not (and cannot) act, but only "in rapt contemplation" behold the action on stage. The chorus provides the element in the drama which presses upon the antagonists in the manner in which the audience presses upon the stage as a whole.[54] In this, it is for Nietzsche the structural device whereby the audience is swept up onto the stage and taken out of itself. Both the chorus and the audience can do nothing about what is happening on stage. They can only behold. This state provides for Nietzsche the basic characteristics of what he calls the "dionysian"; thus *both* the spectators and the chorus are in a "dionysian state."

It is through the medium of the chorus that the audience comes to feel itself part of what occurs on stage. It participates without being a part. This is a complex matter: it seems to go something like this. Relations between the events taking place on stage and the spectators are not reciprocal. The actors-as-characters are in the present of the audience. The reverse is not true, for the audience cannot be in the acknowledged present of the actors. (A familiar fact: the play is broken if an actor talks *with* an audience member.) The players do not recognize the audience, and there is no way in which the audience, as audience, can compel the action on stage to acknowledge it. (This is the source of the omnipotence noted before.)

This deconstruction allows Nietzsche to make sense of exactly how an audience might be transformed. The *Oresteia,* after all, is on one level a trilogy about competing principles of social organization, presented as equal in claim, along with a suggestion as to their resolution. According to Nietzsche's reading of the audience-stage relationship, the audience (who do not relate to the stage in a reciprocated manner) is, by virtue of its dionysian state, swept up onto the stage through the similarly dionysian medium of the chorus. In the same section of the *Birth of Tragedy* Nietzsche writes:

> The proceedings of the tragic chorus is the dramatic proto-phenomenon: to see oneself [as embodied in the chorus] transformed before one's very eyes [as spectator] and to begin to act as if one had actually entered into another body, another character. . . . And this phenomenon is encountered epidemically: a whole throng experiences this magic transformation. . . .(p. 57)

Such a transformation, or at least the seed of it, lasts beyond the moment of theater. For Nietzsche, this is the important social and cultural aspect of the play; the illusion created in the theater and accepted by the audience must be so powerful that it makes a potentially permanent and on-going difference. Likewise a congregation might find itself caught by one of Donne's sermons[55] or a Puritan community might discuss the theological issues for that day's sermon as a matter of immediate practical significance.[56]

It is important to remember that Nietzsche does not find the "message" in, say, Aeschylus, to be centrally important.

The dramatist is not arguing for one side over another; he writes neither plays of propaganda nor dramas of resignation. Indeed, the didacticism implicit in the former is appropriate only in a world where common knowledge is basically secure and in which a writer may then concentrate on matters of practical, as opposed to conceptual, importance. Rather Aeschylus is trying to provide a context for dissolving and making livable the various competing and diverse aspects of the confused moral and political landscape. It is thus not inaccurate to speak of him as attempting to ground, artistically, a new moral community in a sort of new, unquestioned "absolute": a new state from a reborn foundation.

Merleau-Ponty has written eloquently about this process. Speaking of Husserl, he notes that this philosopher used

> the fine word *Stiftung* — foundation, establishment . . . to designate those operations of culture which open a tradition, continue to have value after their historical appearance, and require beyond themselves acts (*opérations*) both other and the same, in which they perpetually come to life again and again. . . . [This tradition is], as Husserl remarks, the power to forget origins, to begin again differently and to give to the past not a survival, which is the hypocritical form of forgetfulness, but the efficacy or repetition of life, which is the normal form of memory.[57]

In such a *Stiftung* the past is annihilated and replaced by a new foundation. Merleau-Ponty is referring to the grounding of a new artistic style of vision, but his remarks apply to the development of any new metaphor or symbolic system that gives us a world. Such a new system is convincing not because it describes the world better, but because at a particular time it gives us a world in which we find our feet. As Clifford Geertz has remarked:

> The power of a metaphor derives precisely from the interplay between the discordant meaning it symbolically coerces into a unitary conceptual framework and from the degree

to which that coercion is successful in overcoming psychic resistances such semantic tension inevitably generates in anyone in the position to perceive it.[58]

An important question appears here. We have seen that there is a possibility of individual resolution and recognition of an identity in the experience of theater. Furthermore, we have seen that this transformation is in an important sense political in that it consists both in the formation of a particular self and in the change away from an "inherited" self, and that this takes place in a collectivity (the audience). We have also seen how the elements of perfection and pretense were central to that experience which allows this to happen. We have not seen, and this constitutes the second important part of Rousseau's criticism, how we can view this transformation as properly *social*. If it remains on the individual level, even on the level of a multitude of individuals, it lacks that element of politics that is concerned with mutual self-recognition. Rousseau writes that although the emotions that occur in stage characters are repeated in members of the audience, the goal of these emotions is not. Thus there is no guarantee that the emotions will retain a common goal. If this is true, theater calls the community and politics into question. Put most bluntly, how much like a character (or a text) is a person?[59]

This issue may seem especially damaging to the approach I have adopted. Following Fish and Vernant (and originally Hegel and Nietzsche), I have indicated that the "content" of a play was not as central to the audience experience as what it *did,* its "work" as Freud would have called it. I have also argued that theater works in a certain manner: Rousseau thought much the same and, for him, this cut against the city.

Much of what Rousseau fears indeed often occurs. Much drama fails to give to the audience a coherent world to experience. Still, in the best drama something else does occur. The difference comes about through the particular quality that great theater can have in resolving the multivoicedness of language in a particular historical period. Let us take these elements in reverse order.

Great drama is typically associated with limited spans in Western history. Vernant and Vidal-Naquet have insisted on the fact that Greek drama knew its true flowering for barely a ninety-year period. The same might be said of Elizabethan drama (as it will also be, I suspect, of the twentieth century). According to Vernant this is related to what one might call the liminal quality of drama.[60] Tragedy flourishes properly in a situation in which a society has changed such that the patterns of the past are beginning to become strait and hardened, yet not to the degree that the past appears impossibly distant and ossified.[61] In Greek drama, for instance, there is an opposition of the human and the divine, but not yet a complete separation. There is a fruitful tension in Aeschylus and Sophocles, which fades in Euripides and, by the time of Thucydides, has vanished almost completely.

The first requirement of truly successful tragedy is then a particular historical situation, itself due to causes external to the theater. The emphasis on language is corollary to this first historical consideration. The audience for the *Oedipus* sees the protagonist enacting one self—that of the man of *tekne*—all the while unaware that he is shaping another self, that of the *pharmakos,* the healing poison, the ritual scapegoat. Likewise in the *Antigone,* the audience sees the performance of the word *nomos* in the actions of Creon and the opposite performance of the "same" word in those of Antigone. The audience is thus presented with two activities of the "same" word that separate individuals from each other in tragic and clearly unacceptable ways. The play shows us, however, what the relation of the two grammars can be. That which had divided the community is now transformed such that the community can come together around precisely that which had divided it.[62] That this resolution is successful can be seen by the radically different manner in which the word *nomos* is treated by Socrates in the *Crito.*[63] Thus it is not quite true, as Rousseau argues, that theater can "create nothing new."[64] Here we have the creation of a world that resolves (for a while, for these people) a situation in which people were unable to know and to admit that they did not understand each other, or, indeed, themselves. For the audience the full and imperfect meaning of the language is (re)created in the drama and, in the words of Gonzalo at the end of *The Tempest*, we may

> . . . rejoice
> Beyond a common joy, and set it down
> With gold on lasting pillars
> . . . [that] all of us [have found] ourselves
> When no man was his own.

Such grounding is the possible result of many, if not all, kinds of dramatic writing. Such situations seem to me to resemble strongly those which Aristide Zolberg analyzed as "moments of madness."[65] These moments occur at early stages of a revolutionary situation when all is felt possible, when the imagination is in power. These are precisely the times when all concerned integrate their life into a new form, indelibly marked by that immediate experience. Anyone who has participated in the various important political movements in Western countries over the last twenty-five years knows what communities were founded and remain resonant from those times. *Stiftung* is an ever-recurrent possibility in times of transformation, when "anything is possible."

IV

My analysis of the experience of drama has led me to evoke a number of political moments which seem to me to reduplicate those moments which we find in the experience of theater. In such moments, politics and drama *are* in fact merged: we have the same experience on the barricades as we do in the theater, when "*l'imagination est au pouvoir*," and humans find, meet, and recognize each other face to face. If, however, this were the only relationship between theater and politics, it would be interesting but not of wide import. As Hannah Arendt has shown us, such points in human time, when external authority has broken down and men and women can meet each other in a transparent and unmediated fashion, must be occasional and cannot live beyond those moments. Typically, neither the moment of authority nor that of collective action is raised or solved. After all, the stuff of politics is not generally the festival of life which we see in those brief times. Politics is rather, as Max Weber once put it, most often the "slow boring of hard boards."

My second major claim is that political philosophy does something more than drama, or at least something that drama cannot do, although drama can point at it and make it possible for us. The centrality of this claim will have to reside in the demonstration that the range of speech and recognition of persons in political philosophy, if perhaps less perfect than it is in drama, is still, in the end, precisely because of those imperfections, greater and more important for us. I propose to investigate this claim by the examination of two portions of two plays by Shakespeare. I am aware of the difficulties of calling up my paradigm cases *ex machina* as it were, but I think that such Aristophanic license may be forgiven me.

More precisely, I wish to look at the question of the play-within-the-play. I wish to claim that the play-within-the-play stands to the rest of the play in the same manner that the play as a whole stands to our ordinary life. In this relation we can see the uses and misuses of theater for life, for it is in the play-within-the-play that the theater confronts life.

Remember then the first scene in *King Lear*. The Earls of Kent and Gloucester enter with Edmund, bastard son to Gloucester. Edmund has apparently been away on military service and is but little known to Kent. Indeed, it appears that Gloucester is in somewhat of a hurry to send him off again. Kent queries if this be Gloucester's son, and is told that such must be acknowledged openly, it having shamefully been brought out so often. Gloucester then avoids the acknowledgment with "Besides there was sport in his making."

We are explicitly in the realm of the recognition and acknowledgment of persons, and more importantly of the world in which the recognition may be or is being compelled. We sense some of the problems of such compulsion in the fact that this conversation takes place with Edmund present, and given the decent Kent's line to Edmund — "I must love you and sue to know you better" — probably with some discomfort (even if well brought off) on Edmund's part. From these thirty lines in prose, the play sweeps on in verse with Lear's entrance. He is in full command of the situation, not at all senile, and is about to stage a ceremony that will formalize succession in the kingdom. He is without male heir. In order to avoid "future strife," he must divide up his kingdom among his three daughters, of whom he prefers the youngest, Cordelia. In turn, in a kind of parody of feudal oaths, each of the older daughters swears total love to him — despite the fact that they are already married. But when it comes to Cordelia's turn, she finds that she cannot "heave her heart into her mouth" in order to gain "the more opulent third" which her father has promised her. Lear is furious, and when she persists, he cuts her off without dowry, and divides the kingdom into two (which is what Gloucester had apparently thought he was going to do.)

Much should be said about this scene,[66] yet two questions rise above the others. First, why is this scene here and why is it played so precipitously? Lear's entrance is majestical and stately; within seventy lines all is in ruins. I suspect it is because this theatricality is what the play is about. Lear is attempting to give his kingdom a theatrical wholeness and grounding, to eliminate what comes before by this one magical moment. This is his "darker purpose." He forces us by the rapidity of the action to ignore all other questions, especially those of prior intent. He takes not only us, but all those around him (some who had thought he might do something else) by complete surprise and begins the world anew.

Second, what is the relation of this scene to the rest of the play? The scene is often thought problematic. Some of the difficulty disappears if we think of it as a play-within-a-play. The scene with his daughters is clearly rehearsed, in Lear's mind, if not in fact. The older daughters play their part to perfection, exactly as Lear had hoped and expected they would. It is Cordelia who shatters the perfection of Lear's play. Now the function of the play-within-the-play, which Goldman argues is present in all drama,[67] is to precipitate some recognition of fact which will lead to the unraveling of a situation previously thought self-contained. The play-within-the-play leads to an action that would not have happened otherwise.

Lear is then trying to mix his worlds, to accomplish the political goal of legitimizing this strange succession situation. This is a theatrical event we are witnessing in scene one and, unless it is staged this way, it makes little sense. It is then a mistake to see Goneril and Regan as insincere, just as it would not make sense to see any actor as insincere, except as a fault in acting. They are acting, playing characters. In this sense, they are no longer characters in the play, but persons taking on characters to fit the particular play Lear is staging. This act — the becoming of a character — is the problem of the play as a whole. Lear requires that his daughters act, pretend, their love for him. This is something that cannot coherently be acted, since they are supposed to love him in fact. The recognition of others which is love is precisely something that cannot be said, only shown and done. (Here we see the strength and limitation of Fish's stylistics.) Reflect for a moment: What do you do when someone says to you "tell me you love me."? Should you acquiesce, the perfection of love is broken; should you say nothing, then all is threatened. In this, being asked to say that you love someone is here somewhat like murdering someone on the stage: it cannot actually be done and still retain the pretense which is necessary for there to be theater. (For one thing the actor cannot be released by applause.) Yet it is precisely theater which Lear would make out of the love of his daughters.

It is this last point that Cordelia understands. What Lear is asking for cannot be said, or at least it cannot be required. She must break the magic and the spell which Lear would create and thus also the pomp and theatricality necessary to his "darker purpose." She takes, in other words, the politics of the situation seriously, for she knows that what her father asks cannot be the stuff of theater, only of life.

Her reaction then is to deny that his question can be a question for theater. She is troubled by the implications of what she is doing, for she recognizes, I think, the difficulties of Lear's political predicament, and when he pushes her, tries to mend her ways and proclaim at least that part of herself which is her theatrical *dramatis persona,* that she is his daughter and loves him as such. That is what it means to be part of the cast list, we might say:

> You have begot me, bred me, loved me. I
> Return those duties back as are right fit,
> Obey you, love you, and most honor you.
> Why have my sisters husbands if they say
> They love you all? Haply when I shall wed,
> The lord whose hand must take my plight shall carry
> Half my love with him, half my care and duty.
> Surely I shall never marry like my sisters
> To love my father all.

This is a good try and Cordelia is reasoning well. But it is not enough. For Lear's succession device to work, only true recognition of another will suffice — this is what he has based his legitimacy principle on. Thus Lear cannot step outside of the world which he has created for himself; indeed, he has already overdetermined it, down to where he shall live, when, and with what retinue. And being himself unable to escape theatricality, he cannot fulfill the political needs he has imposed on himself. The perfected acting demanded by the love test playlet makes the changing world of politics impossible.

So the whole skein comes apart, both the ordinary world and that of the theater. In the end there will be only a partial recognition by Lear of any other — Gloucester in this case — and then it will be too late, whether his politics win or lose. The mixture of roles in his final confused recognition of Cordelia ("For as I am a man, I do think this lady to be my child . . .") indicates that he still does not see the person for the characters and that he has not moved much since the beginning of the play.

Cordelia, we might say, is trying to keep the theater in its place and live in the changing and political world of human beings, of past and present, of future and incompleteness. She recognizes fully the temptations of theater and the ease with which one confuses it with the ordinary world. (Nietzsche was to accuse Wagner of doing this.) Thus she will insist on what perforce will happen to her relation to her father when she marries someone else and on all the contingencies of everyday living. Indeed, I suspect that the very insistence on this theme accounts for the ambiguous reception which *Lear* has had in various ages. In those ages that are secure in themselves, the end appears to be impossibly close to real life: remember Jonson's outrage at the double death of Lear and Cordelia and his desire to put theater back into the play by having them live. In ages more liminal, the play rings particularly true; one can only marvel that Shakespeare managed to create a play about the dangers of theater. His achievement is not equaled until Beckett's *Endgame*.

Breaking the hold of theatricality and the recognition of the separateness of ordinary life is a repeated theme in Shakespeare. At times theatricality breaks on itself or by force of arms, as in *Richard III*. Here one can most easily continue the discussion by looking at a portion of *The Tempest*, traditionally, Shakespeare's last play.[68] The whole island on which the play takes place is a stage, controlled and changed at will by the magician-prince-artificer Prospero. He manipulates events, nature, reality itself to suit his desires and purposes. In this great theater (though it is a bit outrageous to say it), the antitheatrical role of Cordelia is taken on most directly by Caliban, the "deformed slave" whom Prospero had found on the island. It is Caliban who insists on Prospero's past, on the problematics and artifices and manipulations which are central to the exercise of his authority and power. (Prospero's own description of his past to his daughter Miranda is cut off with an admonition that she ask no more and a spell which puts her to sleep: hardly the elements of reciprocity.) It is Caliban who insists on the human, even if he does it in terms both direct and crude, "I would have peopled the isle with Calibans".

Initially the island of *The Tempest* is a world of magic, outside time and the self-consciousness of humanity. Prospero, in fact, is in control of all pasts that anyone there might have. In Act I, ii, he makes sure that Miranda and Caliban and Ariel have the proper understanding of their own past. To control the past is to control the present, indeed, to control mortality itself, and Prospero is highly unwilling to give up this control. He promises, for instance, a half dozen times to release Ariel, always finding for him one important task more.

What *The Tempest* shows us are the limits and problems of this world of perfection and artifice. By the end of Act IV, Prospero has made an explicit decision to use open power against Caliban, to plague him as one person to another, "even unto roaring," and no longer to try to control him. Although this is unpleasant (to put it mildly) for Caliban, it is the first act on Prospero's part which constitutes a recognition of Caliban as a person. And from that point in the play, Prospero refers to Caliban in a different manner. It is no longer "hag see," "vile slave," but "you" and "he." This point marks a transition and shift in Prospero's understanding and recognition of himself. In the next scene, V,i, Prospero is informed by Ariel of the sad lot of the imprisoned part of the off-island ducal company.

> Ariel: Your charm so strongly works them
>   That if now you behold them, your affections
>   Would become tender.
> Prospero: Dost thou think so, spirit?
> Ariel: Mine would, sir, were I human.
> Prospero: And mine shall.

Prospero's response is key. His now recognized ordinary humanity requires that he forgive the prisoners (who have in the past greatly harmed him), and that he refuse the possibility of unbridled power, that he not become Ariel, but return to earth, somewhat closer to Caliban, "This thing of darkness, I acknowledge mine."

If one would be human, there must be a limit, self-imposed for those who live without God, on perfection and immortality. The desire for immortality is allure which leads us to confuse the stage with ordinary life, precisely the same urge that lies at the source of original sin. *It is not that perfection and immortality cannot be attained, but that they can, that forms the human problem.* The stage shows us what we might be like were we accomplished and perfected, were we gods. The refusal of the stage — Cordelia's and Prospero's refusal — makes us human, or at least offers us that possibility.

It is perhaps a bit like this for the audience. We must remember that theater shows us the recognition of persons, but since those involved are all actors, beings of unlimited strength, their self-recognition in no way forces us to the risk of encountering one another. Rousseau is right in one sense then: important and central to the experience of being a member of the audience is the fact that the emotions on stage do not "require anything" of me. But he is wrong in that he does not see that in theater it is precisely that consciousness which informs us also of the nature of the world in which matters *can* be required of us. Theater shows us what it is to be God-like and the dangers of the perfectedness that involves. At the end of *The Tempest,* in his great speech of renunciation, Prospero breaks his staff of power and "deeper than did ever plummet sound" drowns his book of spells. Now almost human, he can move to the front of the stage, in a bold and courageous epilogue.

> Now I want
> Spirits to enforce, art to enchant
> . . . .
> As you from crimes would pardoned be
> Let your indulgences set me free.

What would we do, if we could not clap?

V

It is perhaps a bit like this for us. The world must remain richer than anything "we" make of it. This is the sense of Prospero's self-limitation. The complete melding of the world with text is a great temptation in that it appears to resolve the anxieties and personhood once and for all. Prospero, if he would be human, must return to Milan. And of what will befall him there, nothing is given, nor is it of interest to the play. We know only that "every third thought" will be his grave, only that once again he is limited, parochial, mortal. For it is once the company has "found themselves," in the words of Gonzalo, that Milan becomes possible and necessary, if only to vindicate humanity and allow it a place. Milan permits life in the community, which is not recovered and not renewed. The recognition of persons has always forced one to leave the garden. This is the deep meaning of the Fall in Genesis; it is the theme which governs Jacques's dark wisdom of the ages of man, even if he was sour and alone in the solitude which ensued.

And it is to Milan that political philosophy is addressed. Political philosophy is, after all, about the limits on perfection. It is the particularly human activity because it serves to define and formulate what it means to be a human being with other human beings. It is, of course, true that there are many ways to address the city, of working out the relations between humans who are limited by mortality and time and space. But we should remember that it is precisely because God was *absconditus* — hidden — to humans that politics was possible and necessary to Calvin. Calvin limited humans in one manner; Locke in another, Rousseau in yet a third. In our time, to be human may even require the recognition that we are deprived of the political altogether for some while. (Hannah Arendt once remarked, in the spirit of loss, that this "may not be the time to ask 'who governs?'")

Drama, however, can show us the possibilities and the dangers of moving beyond politcs and why, if we are to be humans with each other, limitations only serve to make our world (in Caliban's words) "rich and strange." Thus, though the theater can lure us away from ourselves, it can also remind us of what those selves are. Drama can show us why such politics and limitations are necessary. But that is only because drama stands beyond us, transcendental to the world of our sense. It is good that we can clap — there is nothing less complete than a performance at which the actors do not appear for curtain calls. We can clap and we should: for only thus will our applause serve to make our drama into our life and our prose.

3. Science and Political Theory as Activities: Understanding the World and the Political

> HAMM: Did you ever think of one thing?
> CLOV: Never.
>
> S. Beckett, *Endgame*

> We read that the traveler asked the boy if the swamp before him had a hard bottom. The boy replied that it had. But presently the traveler's horse sank in up to the girths, and he observed to the boy, "I thought you said that this bog had a hard bottom." "So it has," answered the latter, "but you have not got halfway to it yet." So it is with the bogs and quicksands of society; but he is an old boy that knows it.
>
> H. D. Thoreau
> *Walden*, "Conclusion"

In THE previous chapter I argued that one dissolution of the tensions of the political self was theatricalization, the achievement of the purity of presentness. Being transparently present, all present to an other, with no discrepancy between self and presentation of self is an epiphanic dream that has tempted humans for at least two thousand years.

In what may seem a debased form, this temptation shows up also as the roles that a rationalized society makes available to us. Part of the temptation of rationalization is that it gives me a role in which to appear to others. It makes it possible for me to claim that I am only that which I am doing. If I am present to others simply and only in the manner that my job requires, I have become a kind of stage role. My lines are given, so to speak, and I do not need to know what else to say other than what is in those lines. A sentence like "I'm sorry, sir, but I can't do anything: those are the rules" neatly encapsulates the temptations and the possibilities of hiding as presence.[1]

But the shaping of such roles — the organization of a whole society along such lines — requires that a script be constructed. It requires devising and accepting a future that can be controlled. In this chapter I want to examine not the theatricalized self, but the self that would construct a world such that the self can be theatricalized. We might think of this as the temptation of science, that is, of the idea that we can, should, and must shape what we will be. The motivation is to deal with human suffering — to avoid that which fortune throws our way.

That the alleviation of human problems required a science of human behavior has moved thinkers at least since Machiavelli. It reflects an appreciation of the power of knowledge and of method.[2] Were regularities of human behavior to be discovered and organized according to knowable laws, then the administration of human affairs would no longer be dependent upon humans and their foibles of character and ability. As Hume argued,[3] the demand for a science of human behavior has its origins both in a distrust of the ability of ordinary human beings to know and control themselves sufficiently, *and* in the fear that human beings left to themselves will fall prey to those more clever, more devious, and more evil. If government were of laws and not of men, then no one need depend on the particularities of individuals for their own good. That the laws were themselves man-made and discovered requires that some seek out such a science.

Most of those who sought a science of human behavior, no matter how they defined that term, did so with the understanding that it would have to be a science which reflected the fact that humans were different than "natural" phenomena such as planets, waves, and gravity. Hegel saw this and tried to develop a science of human behavior which recognized that human action contained the terms by which it was understood.[4] Max Weber argued that social science dealt with *meaningful* actions and was in this inherently different from any science that sought general laws.[5] More recently, Alasdair MacIntyre has argued that the knowledge of political scientists is not dissimilar in kind to that of political actors. It is a form of narrative, a story-telling with a beginning, middle, and end. As such the subject matter of politics is moral and simply does not permit lawlike generalizations.[6]

Well, why not? Most often this question has been approached in a manner that seems to me misguided. Two moves are involved: one is a qualitative differentiation between human and other actions, and the second an elaboration of a science particular to human actions. The assumption is that there is a common world (human "nature," the "life-world," architectonic categories of experience[7]) which constitutes a given space in which all humans exist. The delineation and delimitation of this world is the task for the human sciences. The presumption is that we will have accomplished our task when we have referred actions back to a theoretically grasped common world.

I wish to begin my considerations by arguing two things. First is an investigation of the claim that human affairs are different in kind from natural affairs; I do not want to deny that they are different, only that the difference is not basic. We should, in other words, try to understand *how* they become different. Second, and derivatively, I want to argue that the claim that human affairs are different because we all share a primary common space is mistaken. Commonness is achieved, not given.

One approach to differentiation tries to establish a line of cleavage between human and natural phenomena by means of invoking "intentionality." The argument goes something like this. That which illuminates a raised fist as more than a simple piece of behavioral fact is the "intention" that lies "behind" it: depending on what the actor intends, the same gesture becomes a sign of welcome, or an angry warning, or a gesture of proletarian solidarity.[8]

The spatial adverb — "behind" — is telling, even more so when it is replaced by "under." The implication is that intention is something essentially mentalistic, more or less private, more or less graspable, if at all, only by some kind of "empathic" or "hermeneutic" understanding, which is peculiar to human affairs and importantly different from the way in which one understands "real" facts.

This argument is often challenged: harder line behaviorists think that a science of behavior must make no reference to internal processes such as intention; their opponents think that it must.[9]

There are criticisms to be made of both the behaviorist and the "hermeneutic" approaches. Behaviorists fail to recognize that the factuality of that which we know is itself a problem; "hermeneuticists" tend to attribute a magical quality to intention and to conclude that all one can do is interpret rather than explain.[10] I will deal with these questions somewhat more directly in the final chapter, but the important issue here is that the very distinction seems to me flawed. Both sides retain the notion that the human person is divided into two parts, more or less separate and in any case separable, the one inward and "subjective," the other external and "objective."[11] *I wish rather to argue that at a deep level the process by which facts become facts for the political world is not fundamentally different from that by which facts become facts for the physicist, and that neither the world, nor a person, is split into two parts* ("high and low," "surface and depth," etc.). I shall try to show, however, that while the facticity of political science and physics is basically of the same structure, that which goes into the facts in each case is quite different. I wish then to oppose the notion, common to phenomenology and assumed by behaviorism and rational-choice theory, that we "naturally" share a common "life" — which stands prior to our ability to do physics or political science, or anything else. The acts of theorizing and living are much closer to each other than one might have previously supposed.

My approach, then, is to suggest that most often a "science of human affairs," *whether it accepts a qualitative gulf between the human and the natural sciences or not,* has sought to bring human affairs under control. While the desire to bring our affairs under control — that is, to make the future subject to the understanding of the present — has a place, it is always, because of the nature of knowledge, doomed to failure. However, as noted in the previous chapter, understanding this failure is to understand the self that acts in the political world from knowledge.

* * *

One might say in the manner of Wittgenstein that we have political attitudes and behavior if and when we have political facts. We must then begin by asking "what makes a fact a political fact?" We need to explore the factuality of politics by looking at what facts are for rationalized and formalized knowledge, here designated as "science." We also need to explore those facts that political theory deals with by looking at their distance from, tension with, and relations to what count as facts in the world of "science." I shall hold that the division of the political self into "levels," the "deepest" of which might be intentionality, is wrongheaded, and while it is true that the source of meaning is in human activity, what is revealed is not that the self is private but that it is communal. What I am interested in is a problem given its strongest recent formulation by Louis Althusser. We seek to know "whereby a particular discourse functions as [political] knowledge, and not as something else, not as a hammer, symphony, sermon, [or science]. . . ."[12]

The Grammar of Knowledge

As an approach to our grasp of where we are in the world, doubt as a philosophical tool has an honorable history. It is explicit in the dialogue form; it provides a source of health and political wisdom in the Renaissance; in modern times, it finds its classic embodiment in the civilized skepticism of

Hume. It is with Kant, however, that doubt becomes not only civilized, but useful and constructive. In his critical philosophy Kant appears to conclude that Hume had the questions upside down. He tries to turn Hume on his feet again and, instead of seeing what *could* be doubted (which for Hume was everything except statements on the order of "the sum of the interior angles of a triangle is 180 degrees"), Kant seeks to account for *how* we know what we do know. In effect Kant says that humans engage in various actions — they make moral judgments, they reason, they do science — and that the problem is to see what they are in fact doing when they are doing these activities. The effort then is to bring the various actions which make up a life more clearly into light, so that one can be able to know in fact what one is doing. (In this, as in much else, Kant harks back to Socrates: it is not that men and women do not lead lives, but that they do not know what they do when they lead those lives.) Kant shows us that these activities make up our life and what our knowledge of that life and of our world in fact is. He wants to show us what we are doing.

In its most general form, Kant calls this operation a "transcendental deduction." His main point is one we saw in the previous chapter: that knowledge in most of its forms has *limits,* and that these limits are not *faults* in knowledge (which had been the conclusion of Hume and the skeptics), but the very condition of knowledge itself.[13] The knowledge that Kant hopes for us to gain from the investigations pursued in the *Critiques* is not knowledge about the "facts" of the world, but rather knowledge of what we must be or accept *when* (not before) we investigate the "facts of the world." Such knowledge, as Stanley Cavell has remarked, is "meant to provide us [not with] more knowledge of matters of fact, but [with] the knowledge of what would count as various 'matters of fact.'"[14] One might refer to such knowledge as does Wittgenstein, as "grammatical" knowledge, i.e., of knowing what it is right to say, that is, to do, at particular times and places. Grammatical knowledge is not a search for something new, but rather an attempt to describe ourselves and our world when we are involved in a particular activity.

My pursuit here can be thought of as a third cousin to that of the neo-Kantians, who sought to develop a social and historical science explicitly modeled along the lines of the Kantian critiques. Men like Georg Simmel transformed the question of the first *Critique* (How is our knowledge of nature possible?) into a more general socio-philosophical one about actualities (How is Society possible?). They derived a set of abstract interactions which, they thought, constituted the very stuff and limits of society. If we have (what we call) a society, they claimed, then there are *these* interactions.[15]

Having made this parallel, I now wish to differentiate my pursuit from the neo-Kantian approach. The approach we inherit from Dilthey, Simmel, and the others has and continues to have a certain success; it is certainly less culture-bound than the roughly contemporary development of functionalism. Those working in this vein recognized, in a manner that functionalists refused, that perceptions and intentions were an integral part of human interaction. Processes such as intentionality were not just formative of data but are part of them.

There are many problems with the neo-Kantian approach, but one element of truth comes in their recognition that concepts are not simply read off the world like tags on a set of objects. Concepts, indeed, knowledge itself, is intersubjective and can be found *as* human life and activity, not "in" the world. Indeed, following Kant, they understood any attempt to rest knowledge on the "empirical" world alone, as, say, Locke and the British empiricists tried to do, was doomed to failure. As Kant had noted, "Concepts have to be founded on something other than the concrete, or else the whole enterprise is doomed."[16]

Difficulties, on the other hand, come in the fact that the neo-Kantian appreciation of the importance of intersubjectivity as a basis for knowledge is not backed up with a sufficient examination of what the structures of intersubjectivity are, nor how men have them. Thus the categories which Simmel and the others come up with are exceedingly formal and rigid. They portray a fleshless and abstract world, all in the name of humanizing it. Indeed, they raise the question as to whether an intersubjective world so devoid of content might not be meaningless. They provide no satisfying manner to account for how historical men and women might, all the time, recognize themselves and others as particular members of a specific and defined society. The here and now, the parochial, is still a problem for the neo-Kantians: and one finds them and many of the phenomenologists who come out of this tradition falling back on notions such as "empathic understanding" and "grasping."[17]

This is just not our experience. We do, for instance, know not only that persons do not need to agree on what the world is (or what some portion of it is), but more importantly that most of the time we have knowledge of the world that is not the product of agreement and which is specific and meaningful. Most importantly, we know that persons do not have to "intuit" or "empathize" what or how someone else is feeling (or thinking, or knowing) in order to act in meaningful relation to them. This happens in science (we can know what an experiment means) and in everyday life. I do not have to "intuit" your feelings nor engage in "empathic understanding" to know what you mean when you say "I have a toothache" or when you extend your hand to me upon meeting me on the street. There are not two operations involved: I *know*, and there is ordinarily no epistemological space that needs to be filled between what you are "doing" and what you "intend."[18]

The neo-Kantians and the phenomenologists were, it seems to me, overly impressed by the distance between peoples and cultures. Getting to know the other was something like what they thought getting to know a different culture would be.[19] However, as I hope to show below, "getting to know" another, or another culture, does not involve "empathy."

It is important to note that already at this stage the question of intention is *not* normally immediately *raised* by our understanding of activity. By and large, when you come towards me with your hand out (you are my friend, I haven't seen you in three weeks, we went to grade school together), I do not have to ask myself questions about your intentions. It is not that you do not "have" intentions, but that the *question* of them is not raised. Indeed, the meaning of your gesture is so transparent to me that it is *perfectly* clear, and I should find myself surprised, hurt, and expectant of an account of your behavior (you are sick, paying a forfeit, being watched by the Mafia), should you hit me in the jaw rather than shake my hand. Here we might ask with Wittgenstein if, normally, the intention does not "lie also in what [you] did."[20] The point is that to invoke an "intention" that would lie hidden under our action adds nothing to our understanding the relationship.

To assert that I can only understand you if I know your intentions (whether or not I continue to assert that I can or cannot know those intentions) is in fact a way of denying my commonality with you, perhaps with anyone. (As Wittgenstein notes: "[T]he most explicit expression of intention is by itself insufficient evidence of intention."[21]) The pursuit of intentions is thus an expression of estrangement and a demand for a relationship which would be defined by the grasping of (previously invisible) intentions.

The claim that the grasping of intentionality is necessary in all circumstances to understand a human action thus appears as a way of distorting our grasp on the world. It is only when I make a mistake, or when I am fearful, that I begin to wonder about your intentions. (Are they honorable?) Note that the question of intention was not raised under the circumstances of perfect clarity that we examined in the previous chapter. The presumption here is that without an elaboration of intentions human actions will not be immediately visibly clear to others. What is being hidden, such that it will only appear to those who claim to be able to call it forth?

The answer to Wittgenstein's query "does not the intention lie also in what you did?" requires that we see that the closing of the gap between other and self constitutes an acknowledgment of a shared set of practices. And this points at a more preliminary and more accessible lesson. "A grammar of knowledge" cannot be a description of *how to go about* doing (e.g.) science (what intentions you must have), but rather a description of what we are in fact doing when we do (e.g.) science. Kant shows us, for instance, if nothing else, what it means to act morally. Whether or not he shows us in addition what we should do *if we want to be moral,* he certainly tells us what we do in fact when we are moral.[22] A grammar of political theory of the sort for which we are looking will not provide instructions for action, but rather will tell us what (if anything) might count as this particular set of shared practices.

If this contention is admitted, then neither the enterprise of this chapter, nor more generally the proper subject material of the debate about how scientific political science can or should be, *is at all methodological.*[23] I am trying to talk about what it *means to do* political theory. In a similar fashion, much of the debate that surrounded and continues to surround the issues raised in Thomas Kuhn's *The Structure of Scientific Revolutions* misses the main point. Whether or not Kuhn was speaking of how to go about doing science, he was certainly trying to talk about what actually happens when people (whom we call scientists) do (what we call) science.[24] Whether or not the claim that science is cumulative and progressive is a necessary or merely a historical part of what it means to do science seems to me a question that is separable from the question of what it means to do science. It must be asked but it is neither the first nor the last question.

All of this may seem to cast the enterprise of this chapter and of political theory in too modest a panorama. I ask the reader to bear with me a bit here if this view appears initially too strait; here, I hope to show, freedom is found. The plethora of images, approaches, variable testing, models, metaphors, and methodologies that presently thicken the journals may very well be a sign of the disappearance of some of the reasons that persons pursue understanding. One probably needs to focus on method when one does not often encounter that which doing science or political theory can give us: the pleasure of agreement; the excitement of knowledge; the joys of discovery.[25] That we often do not experience these feelings is a partial sign that we may not be able to recognize political theory or science in the world around us. For, I wish to argue, *having these experiences is what we mean by a grammar of knowledge.*[26]

The Problems of Perception

I suggested above that a science is an activity and a form of communication and that it reposes, as do all other human activities and communications, on a communal structure, a "we." I have claimed that the apprehension of this structure is a matter of life, of activity, that is, of having certain experiences with others, and not of grasping "subjective" mental processes, of moving from the "outside" to the "inside." It is now time to explore these claims more fully and, especially, to determine to what sort of world they correspond.

I take it as true that, since Kant, (crude) empiricism is no longer a tenable position. We no longer think—at least we should no longer think—that understanding the world is merely a matter of opening our eyes and hearing the unproblematic message of the "facts." I shall not expand on this any further, except to note that the metaphor is consciously mixed. But some of the consequences of this for our understanding of science will appear obvious and a truism; others may appear more contentious. Whether the reader encounters this next section as a reminder or argument I trust it will be helpful.

First, science does not live by observation alone, at least if one means by "observation" that what a scientist has to do is to *find* facts. There is more involved in science than simply acquiring information. Alexandre Koyré notes that the simple empiricist approach may hinder the advance of science, for "it is only when subjected to theoretical treatment that knowledge of facts becomes science. Besides, observation and experience—in the meaning of brute commonsense observation and experience—have a very small part to play in the edification of modern science; one could even say that they constituted the chief obstacles they encountered on its way."[27]

The reasons are obvious. Observation alone will not tell us *which* facts count, nor, more importantly, *exactly what counts as a fact.* "It is," writes Stephen Toulmin, "simply irrelevant to criticize earlier scientists for blindness. . . . If they sometimes seem to have shut their eyes to the facts, we need to ask: 'could the things which we regard as "facts" have been certain, clear or even intelligible to earlier investigators?'"[28] The claim is not that a scientist somehow missed seeing what was important, but that his first problem was to determine what would count as important, i.e., to respond and be provoked. If the world is always more than we make of it, then the making of *some-*thing of it — which is what science is — can only be a determination of what will count as part of the world we make. To some great degree, a theory will let an investigator know what will count as proof and disproof. (This is not totally true — even if we can say anything we want, we can only want some-thing — but the reasons for it will have to wait.) For instance, it would seem wrong to suppose that repeated experimentation will *by itself* determine what is true. Nelson Goodman reminds us that we do not even know what we mean by the "same experiment" without at least some sort of preexisting partial theoretical structure.[29]

This is a complex matter taking us not only to the heart of the activity of science but informing us on what it means to be a human being in the world. We are approaching it by the route of the question of the status of the "subject" in general. When it is a question of knowledge, what is the relation of the mind/subject/perceiver to that which it knows/has for object/perceives? It is true that we can reflect on our perceptions. It was, however, the central achievement of Bishop Berkeley to have shown that even the conceptual distinction between observation and ideas about observation was misleading. We cannot eliminate the effects of observing from that which is observed, nor should we want to, for these "effects" are the stuff of what we mean by observation.[30]

A first example: There is no way I can keep myself from seeing the duck-rabbit as either a duck or a rabbit (assuming I know what ducks and rabbits are). Whatever I see, I inevitably see *as something*. To see "as something" means not just to see something "in a context," but that there is no seeing that is not contextual.[31] Context is (part of) what we mean by seeing. Thus when we speak of an observation we are also speaking of a context. What something *is* cannot be separated from the context in which it is a fact. It is not clear what it would actually mean to make a clear-cut distinction between observation and context.

While overall most of our life is relatively context invariate, there is no reason to assume that there is one and only one context in which a stimulus was a datum. W. V. O. Quine remarks that "reference is nonsense except relative to a coordinate system"[32] and we know this to be true even of reflex systems.[33] If we have learned anything from Gestalt psychology, it is that perceiving is an active and form-making process. As Nietzsche knew in his doctrine of the will-to-power, it is a making of the world, though this making need not be just as one wants or expects.[34]

A second example: In the seventeenth century Hobbes and Boyle quarreled over Boyle's argument that his experiments with his newly invented airpump demonstrated the existence of a vacuum in nature. A wide range of issues was involved. Boyle claimed that metaphysical arguments were irrelevant and cited experimental proof in his favor. Hobbes retorted that Boyle's device leaked, and that all Boyle could do was to *assert* that what he had discovered was a vacuum. To the notion of experimental proof, Hobbes responded that the claim of authority that there was a vacuum could not be resolved purely on an observational basis. One cannot simply *decide* to jettison "metaphysics."[35]

I shall return to the Hobbes-Boyle case in more detail later but this initial point continues the above argument. I have asserted that there is no obvious one-to-one correspondence between what is "in the world" and what we perceive when we are in the world. I have also denied that perception is simply a matter of filtering stimuli through some sort of mental grid. But in addition to the impossibility of a sense-datum language, *there is no such thing as having just one experience.* In a major article, "Empiricism and the Philosophy of Mind," Wilfred Sellars dealt with this problem in great depth. I cite at length:

> For if the ability to recognize that X looks green presupposes the concept of *being green,* and if this in turn involved knowing in what circumstances to view an object to ascertain its color, then, since one can scarcely determine what the circumstances are without noticing that certain objects have perceptible characteristics — including colors — it would seem that one could not have the concept of green, and by parity of reasoning, of the other colors, unless he already had them.
>
> Now it won't do just to reply that to have the concept of green, to know what it is for something to be green, it is sufficient to respond, when one is in point of fact in standard conditions, to green objects with the vocable "This is green." Not only must the conditions be of the sort that it is appropriate for determining the color of an object by looking, the subject must know that conditions of this sort are appropriate. [This is the point about the theory-ladenness of observation.—TBS] And while this does not imply that one must have concepts before one has them, it does imply that one can *have the concept of being green only by having a whole battery of concepts of which it is one element.* It implies that while the process of acquiring the concept of green may, indeed does, involve a long history of acquiring piecemeal habits of response to various objects in various circumstances, there is an important sense in which one has *no* concept pertaining to the observable properties of physical objects in Space and Time unless one has them all — and indeed as we shall see a great deal more besides.[36]

I shall leave Sellars's promissory note at the end untouched, but enough has been said to shed some light on our concerns. Most generally, for Sellars, there are no concepts which do not presuppose a whole realm of discourse. One can never know, or say, just *one* thing; to know anything at all means to assert one's membership in a world already inhabited by the enactments of others. This world may be very simple, as in the world of chess, or as formally complicated as etiquette, or as mysterious as marriage; but know one part of it, and the rest is present with that part. It is *complete* in the sense that it does not present itself to us as unfinished, no more than did the world as theater. (Of course, we may deny that we do know, but that is a move in terms of the world.[37])

Next, a world is acquired "piecemeal," that is, presumably, it is learned, mainly through the experience of having knowledge of meanings which allow the world to be meaningful in the terms of these meanings. (If you know what green is, you know what a color is, and you will only have vocabulary problems with puce.) This points at the most important insight of Sellars's text, namely that the "whole battery of concepts" makes possible knowledge of "specific" facts. In other words, to know anything at all presupposes that one belongs to a community of discourse that is public, can be learned, and is not in principle inaccessible to other individuals.[38]

If this general conclusion is accepted—and a great deal more sophisticated argument might be adduced from the writings of Wittgenstein[39]—a number of conclusions can be drawn as to what knowledge is. First, no concept can be defined with such absolute precision as to make it perfectly clear once and for all *exactly* what that concept is.[40] For instance, we know generally what sorts of things count as voting; do we want to call the process by which candidates are elected to the Supreme Soviet "voting"? There is no answer to this except case by case; generally, the only correct answer is "it is often hard to say." We know by and large what sorts of states count as death, except in those cases that medical technology now enforces on us.[41]

The important point is not the justification of an exuberant anarchistic brio, but the claim that it is in the nature of the categories by which we understand the world (and each other) not to have sharp boundaries. The drawing of categories should thus be done with an eye to their natural porosity. T. S. Kuhn proposes the case of a child who is faced with the problem of distinguishing among several types of waterfowl. After coming up with swans, geese, and ducks (with the aid of a knowledgeable adult), Judy is obliged to figure out what the limits of goosedom are. How constraining should the definition be? (As in a famous problem: "what about that black swan anyway?") Kuhn proposes that Judy draw the boundaries in such a manner that if, suddenly, a goose should be discovered which barely fits the limits of recognized gooseness — it bulges the existing limiting curve of Judy's perceptual space — the boundary could then be set a little further out, and that appropriate alterations be made in other definitions, so that some conceptual space continue to exist between geese and, say, ducks. Kuhn refers to this as "the learned perception of similarity" and suggests that it is strongly analogous to the manner in which scientists operate.[42]

The most basic point of the above analysis is Kuhn's suggestion that science is learned in somewhat the same way that language is learned, and that one goes through stages of acquiring a vocabulary. Essentially, both here and in his better known *The Structure of Scientific Revolutions,* Kuhn seems to be asking: Where do our categories come from anyhow? His answer might be a paraphrase of Mao Zedong: Scientific categories do not fall from the sky; they come from scientific practice and from scientific practice alone.[43] It is key to Kuhn's analysis that "experience can demand some adjustment of class boundaries." Class boundaries are learned, and learned through the practice of doing science (or in this case, of figuring out about waterfowl).

Doing science, however, does not spring fully grown from the scientist; a good deal of it consists in learning to interact (talk, communicate, argue, agree, disdain, conclude) with other scientists. This is what Kuhn calls "normal science" and it clearly forms for him the most important part of the activity of science. Being a scientist presupposes that one has become a member of a particular group of people who are (what we call) scientists. Since for Kuhn, as for Sellars and Frederic Waisman, scientific laws are, in the words of Merleau-Ponty, not "given by the facts [but] expressed by them,"[44] it is not only my activity that makes me a scientist, but as much my participation in a common, shared world of (scientific) discourse that makes me one. As Sellars remarks, "to recognize a featherless biped or a Martian or dolphin [or a scientist] as a person is to think of oneself and it as belonging to a community."[45]

"Belonging to a community": knowing oneself or an other is the recognition of a community, of the first-person plural pronoun. I have arrived at a point which requires modification, or at least blunting, of my initial claim. From the above brief discussion of Kant and the neo-Kantians, it might have appeared that the aim of this chapter was to uncover (re-cover, dis-cover) *the* transcendental deduction of political and scientific knowledges. Indeed, for Kant, the preconditions of reason were universally and necessarily true. Yet I have just argued that these preconditions are, to some considerable extent, learned through activity and experience. I have suggested that a considerable portion of that which makes up science is shared knowledge and is learned knowledge. (Scientific) knowledge was thus not deducible from the "facts" themselves, because the very existence of these facts presupposes the activity of a particular (scientific) theoretical community.[46] Any community will have a grammar of knowledge and thus of action which serve to define what it is and how it stands in the world. The world of chess, for instance, is made up of certain rule-defined activities, which must be learned and acknowledged if one is to be part of that community.[47] The point is that all such communities will be historical, temporary, and, without calling them into question, parochial.

The particular nature of these communities needs to be explored further. First, I must meet this obvious objection:

> You are unfair to Kant and his position. In the first *Critique,* Kant is seeking to establish what has to be the case when we reason. The things-in-themselves which you have been so busy trying to make historicized and learned, and thus, relativized, are such presuppositions. Granted that

there are times when humans do *not* reason. But if they reason, they do use such *a prioris*. For instance, Kant shows that even though we cannot establish that every event has a cause, we can deduce through the transcendental argument that nature must (does) obey causal laws. Even though these laws are not directly apprehensible, that we think at all shows their validity. This is the starting point that Kant provides. Language is of a piece and there are not several schemas through which we might get meaning.[48]

Such an objection obviously carries a powerful thrust. We do think and reason and understand each other. To deny this is to deny the reality of a large portion of our lives, scientific and ordinary; it raises surreal adolescent anxieties such as "no one ever (really) understands each other." I think, though, that Kant (and Davidson), having discovered he could save the baby, felt obliged also to retain the bathwater. He found that he could account for much of our experience, but he felt that this rendering would not be secure unless the *a prioris* he discovered were given a universal and permanently valid status.

In countering this, I do not want to claim that Kant should be abandoned, but rather emphasize that the world we are investigating, that is, the world of science, itself provides us with these categories. Let us speak rather with Ian Hacking of diverse "styles" of thought, or possibly with Michel Foucault about an *archive*.[49] Hegel's critique of Kant, for instance, admits with Kant that the recognition that the "world" does in fact provide the categories of thought, but adds that the "world" is inextricably bound up with acting persons and is thus richer than the concepts that anyone has of it at any time. Hegel thus calls on Kant not to try and escape the world, but to remain more fully in it. Nietzsche and Heidegger were to continue down this path.[50]

Why Isn't This Crazy?

Somewhere in the course of debates like the above — which have become all too familiar in all the sciences — the question of rationality comes up. Some accusation like this is made: "So you think that science is irrational, that anything goes. You are as bad as . . . as Paul Feyerabend." Now it is true that Feyerabend seems to want to claim that science has irrational components, and if this is his position, I wish to disagree with him. I wish to disagree in any case with the general accusation, though it is clear that if Feyerabend did not exist he would have to be invented.

I propose rather that rationality, including "scientific rationality," be understood to contain an element of a shared and learned world. It is "knowing what to do when." For instance, part of the training in any science seems to consist in being taught what moves to make when confronted with situation *X*. Students are taught what Galileo did with the balls on an inclined plane, why we should not use open fifths in composition, what to do to figure out how the force of gravity affects the curvature of light, what the independent and dependent variables are in Barrington Moore's analysis of the *Social Origins of Dictatorship and Democracy*, etc. A significant part of learning how to be a scientist, that is, how to be the member of a community of discourse, is learning what to do when, of enacting a membership.[51] It is true that in looking back on experiments or in formalizing them, systems of formal rules have been evolved. But it does not follow from this that the one is reducible to the other or equivalent to the other any more than playing squash is reducible to the rule book. We cannot play chess without knowing the rules but knowing the rules is not the same as playing chess. (This does not mean, of course, that they are without relation to each other. These are not two manners of describing the same event with a different degree of sophistication; they are two manners of knowing.[52] Nor is this a case of theory and practice: the two knowledges are too bound up in each other.)

It is worth noting in passing that the position I am proposing is not that ordinarily connected with the writings of phenomenologists such as Alfred Schutz, nor with what is now called "hermeneutics." I am not saying that there is a world of intersubjectivity experience and/or meaning which is prior in some fashion to our "scientific world," and that the latter rests on the former.[53] Rather, I am asserting that these two modes of experience — "voices" in Oakeshott's terminology — co-exist, but do not bear a hierarchical relationship to each other. *They are both entire and to have them both, i.e., to be a scientist and a father and a lover and a citizen (which is or, I gather, should be a normal state of affairs) is a bit like being multilingual,* which all of us, I note, are.[54]

With this, the charge of irrationality is as much beside the point as if it were made of a bilingual person. Israel Scheffler accused Kuhn of "holding a position in which independent and public controls are no more, communication has failed, the common universe is a delusion, reality itself is made by the scientist, rather than discovered by him."[55] It should be apparent, even without Kuhn's subsequent clarifications, ameliorations, and elaborations that this judgment proceeds not only from a fundamental misunderstanding of what Kuhn thinks himself to have accomplished, but also from a lack of comprehension of what is involved in communication and common universes. Scheffler and others in the same vein hold to the position that rationality and science consist in the progressive acquisition of knowledge of the pieces of the jigsaw puzzle of nature. In this view, Kuhn's emphasis on "competing paradigms" certainly appears irrationalist. It would seem that there is no correct picture for the puzzle and that the pieces can be wedged together just as the scientist sees fit.

Now the issue raised here is an important one. The accusation against Kuhn and the others is normally phrased as "irrationalism." This seems to me wrong in that what they are really upset about is the claim of an irresponsible all-powerfulness on the part of the theorist. It seems as if the theorist can call the world anything he wants to. Yet this is precisely what Kuhn and the others are trying to avoid.

What Kuhn does deny is that the universe is ready-made, out there, complete with rationality, ready for taking by the scientific explorer.[56] *He rather insists that scientific rationality lies in the community of scientists and consists of what scientists do when they are doing science.* As Paul Feyerabend notes: "Our present inquiry is not whether there are limits to reason; the question is where these limits are situated."[57] The move here is to determine what the limits of scientific discourse are so as to know when it is approaching a transition area into the realm of, say, politics, or religion, or philosophy.[58]

One way of reading Kuhn then is to say that he and the other so-called "irrationalists" enjoin us to a more limited — I would say, in terms of the previous chapter, more human — form of knowledge, one in which we refuse the temptation to read our present mode of exploring the world as if it were universal. My argument here is that science "works" — that is, men and women can and do do it — but that the notion of rationality, which we have come to associate with science since the explorations of the Enlightenment, needs change. Kuhn sees rationality as knowing-what-to-do-when and as a learned process.[59] Acquiring rationality in science consists in developing and expressing membership in a community of discourse appropriate to the particular task that faces that community. As Alan Blum has remarked:

> Theorizing does not create community, but affirms it; theorizing is not guided by the desire to establish a community of speakers and hearers, but by the Desire to expose its self same commitment to a conception of that which makes speaking and hearing intelligible as the speaking that *is* hearing. Theorizing does not bring speakers and hearers together but affirms their togetherness in its very act of speaking.[60]

The argument is that when we make claims to knowledge we make those claims from a (necessarily limited) community of discourse which preexists and which we have either naturally (through socialization) or explicitly (through choice and training) or necessarily (by remaining alive with others) joined. Any such community is governed by those forms of behavior which define it. And an activity such as doing science or political science is necessarily the affirmation and expression of the meaning of one's membership. Wilfred Sellars has written:

> The fundamental principles of a community, which define what is 'correct' or 'incorrect', 'right' or 'wrong', 'done' or 'not done', are the most general common *intentions* of that community with respect to the behavior of members of the group. It follows that to recognize a featherless biped or dolphin or Martian as a person requires that one think thoughts of the form 'We (one) shall do (or abstain from doing) actions of the kind A in circumstances of kind C'. To think thoughts of this kind is not to classify or explain, but to *rehearse an intention.* [61]

"Intention" in Sellars's usage does not refer to an underlying *explanans,* but only to that which we share with others, such that we know what we mean when we say something. It is because we have a limited mode of action that we have (a particular) meaning. By extension, should we lack that community, we would lack the ability to rehearse those intentions that make our action meaningful and possible; to the degree that we lacked a particular community of discourse — we were not members, or it did not exist — we would not be able to make that kind of sense of the world. Hannah Arendt has argued that the Greek vision of the political is very different (and more pure) than the modern one. So much is obvious, and not exactly news. What is missed, however, in the thrust of her argument is the contention that we have *lost* some aspect of what it means to participate in a community that makes meanings political. This is a problem which fascinated both Kierkegaard and Nietzsche. [62]

What Is Out There Then?

I have tried to establish that (scientific) rationality involves knowing what to do when, and that this is a learned ability. (I grant that humans cannot learn just anything, but this tells us something about humans, not about what they learn.) I indicated that learning how to do science involves joining a community of discourse and that therefore it was somewhat analogous to learning a language. I further indicated that configurations of stimuli do not automatically resolve themselves into a particular and given event: the world is always more than we can make of it *and* always something we have made of it. This is not a subjectivist position: What would it mean to say that a worldview was "simply a matter of belief"? Knowledge is also not just a matter of people getting together and agreeing. (What would they agree about? Why?)

We are almost ready to ask in what way the community of intentions which does natural science is unlike that of politics. It is at this point, however, that a forceful Jonsonian counterargument is raised, in the physical sciences as well as in the social. It runs something like this:

> You say that there are different ways of formulating an event, that it is all a matter of perspective, or at least that there is no one correct perspective. This means that you want to give dominance to the theoretical act. Yet this can't be right. Perhaps you have in mind something like N. R. Hanson's example of Tycho and Kepler viewing the rise of the sun.[63] Hanson may be correct that the experience means something different to each of them; but he is wrong in that he seems to refuse to admit that Kepler is right that the earth moves around the sun and that Tycho is wrong to think the reverse. And, in any case, there is no way that you can convince anyone that there is not something which is the sun-coming-into-sight-in-the-direction-of-Cathay for both of them, no matter what "interpretation" they place on it. All this hermeneutic insight is at best unnecessary. Likewise in social science, it may be that people differ in their interpretation of the trial of the seven demonstrators in relation to the events in Chicago in 1968, but this does not mean that they are not talking about the same event. Psychology may be concerned with why people see what they see, but science is concerned with discovering what really goes on.[64]

Perhaps the thrust of this objection does in fact miss the point, but the motivation behind it has something irreducibly correct to it. Two people may be looking at the Gestalt figure of the duck-rabbit, the one seeing it as a duck, the other as a rabbit. Perhaps they argue about it; but they would be in very different worlds if one wanted to talk about the cotton content of the paper.[65]

This debate has occupied a great deal of time in the philosophy of science since the publication of Kuhn's work, such that it is even easy to refer to "post-Kuhnian thought."[66] The issue at hand has something to do with the relationship of theoretical discourse to the substance of the discourse. Hanson, Kuhn, Feyerabend, Toulmin, and others do often appear to take the position that the theoretical act is architectonic to how the world appears. Israel Scheffler, Ernst Nagel, the early and middle C. G. Hempel, Adolf Grünbaum, and May Brodbeck, all hold that theory is informed and changed by reality and that the world thus contains the terms of its own truth.[67]

This is an extended question and only a few things can be remarked on here. Let us say that I see the duck-rabbit as a rabbit. (I can also be shown that it can be seen as a duck and then amuse myself by switching contexts back and forth.) Here, I want to agree with Sellars that "the idea that sense contents exhibit a lawfulness which can be characterized without placing them in a context of either persons and physical things or of microneurological events is supported only by the conviction that it must be so if we are not to flaunt 'established truths' about meaning and explanation."[68] Thus it is not only "sun" or "rabbit" that are affected by the context. The context is also the theory. The "meaning of a theoretical structure" is the context. It is not just that clocks are understood differently in special relativity or classical mechanics. It is rather that duration is a different entity in each theory. Feyerabend remarks: "The concept of length as presupposed in classical mechanics and the concept of length presupposed in special relativity are different concepts. Both are relational concepts . . . but relativistic length . . . involves an element which is absent from the classical concept and is in principle excluded from it. It involves the relative velocity of the object concerned in some reference system."[69]

One has to move slowly for fear of falling in the idealist trap of positing a structure with no content. In the second part of the *Philosophical Investigations,* Wittgenstein gives an interesting and detailed consideration of this problem:

> I see two pictures, with the duck-rabbit surrounded by rabbits in one, by ducks in the other. I do not see that they are the same. Does it follow from this that I see something different in the two cases?

He gives an oblique answer:

> It gives us a reason [*Grund*] for using this expression here.[70]

Seeing the duck-rabbit as a duck is a *reason* for *using* the expression "I see something different each time." What does this mean? It takes seventeen pages for Wittgenstein to begin to find an answer available:

> Do I really see something different each time, or do I only interpret what I see in a different way? I am inclined to say the former. But why?—To interpret is to think to do something; to see is a state.
>
>   Now it is easy to recognize cases in which we are *interpreting.* When we interpret, we form hypotheses, which may prove false. . . .[71]

Wittgenstein is asking why *I* am *inclined* to say the former. As I read these passages, Wittgenstein's position is that our experience with the duck-rabbit is *more like* seeing something different than it is like interpreting. We do not feel that we are testing the form of the rabbit; there is no real possibility of calling the rabbit into question, hence there is nothing to falsify or prove. It is thus not the case that when we see the rabbit we are seeing something different but that when we see it the foundations of that which make a rabbit available for us are not called into question.[72]

It is also the case, however, that the possibility of my seeing the duck-rabbit as a duck (not as I now see it, as a rabbit) inheres in the seeing of it as a rabbit. Thus while that which makes it a rabbit seems to stand firm it is always questionable.[73]

This presumably means that any community of investigation reposes on shared characteristics which define that community and make it what it is. It stands as true; the condition of it so standing is that it can change. That this is true not only of physics and mathematics but also of language is, I take it, the basis of Wittgenstein's concern with language games; that it is true of politics I take to be the point of Rousseau's elaboration of the general will. Now for some enterprises this community is well established and defined. For others, *less so:* I take this lack to be the basis of Plato's difficulties with justice. In all cases, an investigation of the particular community of discourse, of its strengths and weaknesses, its powers and failures will be an investigation of those people who make up that community—who they are when they do what this community does. Wittgenstein's thoughts now move him to this:

> But mathematical truth is independent of whether human beings know it or not! — Certainly the propositions 'human beings believe twice two is four' and 'twice two is four' do not mean the same. The latter is a mathematical proposition; the other if it makes any sense at all, may perhaps mean: human beings have arrived at the mathematical proposition. The two propositions have entirely different uses. — But what would this mean: 'Even though everyone believed that twice two was five, it would still be four.'? *For what would it be like for everybody to believe that?* — Well I could imagine, for instance, that people had a different calculus, or a technique which we should not call 'calculating'. But would it be wrong? (Is a coronation wrong? To beings different from ourselves it might look extremely odd.)[74]

This is a very complex passage. Reflect, for instance, on the sense of "human beings very different from ourselves" and the implication that not being able to doubt that twice two is four tells us something about what it means to be human—but tells us what? One thing that seems clear is the contention that to know that twice two is four is part and parcel of what human beings do when they do mathematics, and *vice versa*. Being sure of this sum is being part of a "community bound together by knowledge and education."[75]

The point can be extended. One would not know how to doubt that twice two is four and still be doing what is called mathematics. The question could not be raised and this could be not blindness but good sense. The inability to express doubt about some set of propositions (not a fixed set, but one with at least as much permanence as a river bed) is a prerequisite for any activity.

I am not saying here that humans have "agreed" to do mathematics, or physics, or God help us, political theory. This would be silly, like arguing that people agreed to make up the English language. Such worries are left over from our utilitarian forefathers who could not imagine community without individual interests. (Not that these are excluded — *of course* everyone benefits; but we do not have society *so that* each person benefit.) Among the things that humans do together (have done, could do) is political science. To ask why people do political theory, or what political theory is, is then to inquire into a portion of the human condition at a particular time and in a particular place. It is to find that the world of doing political theory and political science is our world and not, again in Sellars's words, "an alien appendage to the world in which we do our living."[76]

Hence the rehearsed and shared enactments which form the basis of human activity, which, in fact, make human beings human, are themselves communal. Action involves sharing a community of discourse, a community which by definition must exist independently of any one individual. Therefore, to think of "intentions" as subjective and purely personal is wrong, and can probably be attributed to adolescent overvaluation of "independence," or to a sense that one's autonomy would somehow be threatened were one not to be finally alone. Wittgenstein argues persuasively that though one can define words as one pleases, one cannot make them mean whatever one intends.[77] This is true precisely because in definition one takes a word out of one context and reintroduces it artificially into another. The intention lies in what one does: for something to have *meaning*, it has to be other than "subjective," otherwise it would be inhuman. "We" have intentions, before I can have any.

How Do We Get to There from Here?

How then does one become part of a community of perception and discourse such as physics or political theory? It seems clear from the above that the necessary ground is not given or fixed once and for all.[78] In an effort to clarify some of his earlier claims Kuhn addressed this problem in his contribution to the symposium on his and Sir Karl Popper's works.[79] He explicitly denies that a shift such as that between classical mechanics and special relativity is made on the basis of "mob psychology," or "taste" indeed, of anything irrational. He then proceeds to identify the sort of things which for scientists constitute the core of their work. He lists these as *accuracy, scope, fruitfulness, simplicity.* He asserts that these hold in science as values, not as rules. Two scientists can and do differ as to what fulfills these values in practice. It is not always obvious which approach is more fruitful, which more accurate, and so forth.[80] Together these values form what Ludwig Fleck called a "thought style . . . a common reverence for an ideal — the ideal of objective truth, clarity and accuracy."[81] *258376*

These structures are at once descriptive and normative of the activity of scientific knowing in general, not just of physics. They are what Stanley Cavell has called "categorical descriptives."[82] They function in relation to scientific knowing much like statements like "Bishops move on the diagonals" function is chess. One simply has no other option; in fact, no other option is presented to us. One cannot imagine (what one would call) a scientific theory which was not (what one would call) fruitful. So also one would not know what to do with someone who claimed to be playing chess and used the bishop only to jump over other pieces.

This claim calls out some obvious objections. First, if the intentions rehearsed in scientific rationality do not have the force of rules, but are rather categorical descriptives which do not necessarily lead to any one definite or enforceable conclusion, does this not imply that history is the final judge of what science is? Second, why do people continue to hold interpretations that must be judged at some moment odd?

As noted before, the first question raises the possibilities of suspicious resonances between this position and those of Hegel, Marx, Nietzsche, and even Foucault. To this, it seems best squarely to admit the links.[83] Hindsight and only hindsight confines a large number of positions to a scientific ash-heap, though not to a graveyard as shown in Heisenberg's recognition of his debt to Anaximander. In retrospect, I suppose that it is true that history (provisionally) decides: I am not sure what else it might do. (Some of this is explored in the next chapter.) Science, I want to say, does proceed rationally, but it is not necessarily clear at any moment what exactly is involved in being rational (or irrational). By and large then, scientific reorientations do not arise from the discovery of new data which would force men to change their minds. Rather they arise from the acceptance, always complicated in terms of the above values, of an elaboration of a manner of looking at the world that is more powerful.[84] "Powerful" has something to do with what humans are trying to make of the world *and is thus not always immediately compelling to everyone.* For instance, the acceptance of the claim that the earth rotated around the sun posed in its initial form a whole host of new problems. Among them was the fact that it was very difficult to account for the observation that bodies fell in a straight line towards the earth; a compensatory theory of a multitude of invisible rectifying angels was briefly entertained.[85]

Why then might a scientist be compelled to make such a switch? From a logical or moral reason, there is no reason at all. The history of science is full of such cases, some of them fruitful, some of them not. Lorentz, whose transformations provided the mathematical formulations for some of special relativity theory, remained a convinced believer in the ether until his death many years after the general acceptance of special relativity. Einstein refused to the end to accept Heisenberg's demonstration that the position and speed of some elementary particles were *in principle* not simultaneously determinable, i.e., that no better theory could be hoped to be found. This refusal, however, made possible Schrödinger's wave equation. Max Planck once noted that old theories are not disproved, they merely die as their proponents do. This *bon mot* is, I think, accurate: it does not imply some sort of irrational process, but rather that it gradually becomes true that to do science is (now) to do it like this. By the mid-1920s for instance, and for an indeterminate period yet to come, it becomes very difficult to do physics if one does not accept most of the tenets of relativity theory. The community moves on in terms of the values that make it a community: I must note that I do not think that this is bad, only that there is no other way for science, or political theory, to function. This is what we mean by "progress."

These values form a structure of intentions that govern the activity of scientific rationality. They form the basis on which scientists modify their knowledge of what to do when. The list is obviously not complete and can certainly be modified; it may be found partially or *in toto* in other communities of discourse. It is to this community that we refer when we point to a set of statements about the world and call them "scientific." When we look at science as a community of discourse and activity, it is to such values that we are referring. It is true that those who do science sometimes, perhaps frequently, operate and speak as if their problems were posed and their solutions given in and by the nature of things. Rational reconstruction is always possible, if only because the operation of science is rational, even if not in the sense of rationality that the proponents of rational reconstruction want to use. There is an important and interesting question in why people have the need to assert that their behavior is *governed* by abstract principles of rationality. Merleau-Ponty, for instance, refers to "the resolution to ignore the meaning which men have themselves given their action" and see it as "the boldest sort of judgment" since it imposes "a priori the categories of the objective historian."[86] Yet this sort of description can never be of the activity itself. In retrospect, Newton appears to have carried the day because his theories were "correct." Yet if we examine the man himself, such a judgment corresponds neither to the opinions others had of Newton, nor to those he had of his own activity.[87]

Science and Political Science

Thus far I have been talking of the nature of communities of discourse and action, in particular of that of science, and have attempted a description of the grammar of knowledge which forms the community of those engaged in what we call science. I have gone to some lengths to establish the claim that the attempts to make sense of the natural world (science) and of the political world (politics) have the same basic structure. I have also been denying that there are "two cultures,"[88] and suggesting that the attempt to impose them is a temptation to which one should not yield.

This, however, cannot be the end of the quest. That science and political reflection have the same structure does not mean that they are identical, even if certain movements inside political science might hold this out as an ideal. The question that now needs to be raised is about the difference of the communities to whom political theory is addressed and that to which science is addressed. It is clear that studying a problem "scientifically" is a way of pointing attention at certain values; it is also a way of establishing what group will have the ultimate say as to what counts as an enhancement of those values. What difference does it make that we try to look at a political question "scientifically?"

To approach this question let us look again for a moment

at a controversy in which these two communities come together in a clash. I refer to the controversy between Hobbes and Boyle over the airpump in the 1660s and the early 1670s.[89] Hobbes, it is often forgotten, was one of the most famous natural philosophers in the seventeenth century, ranking with Descartes and Gassendi. Boyle, of course, was a practitioner of systematic experiment and the inventor of, *inter alia,* the airpump, a device generally thought to have proved conclusively the possibility of the existence of a vacuum. What is important, however, about Boyle's achievement is that, "he did not so much solve the problem of the production of a vacuum as propose a way of avoiding the problem,"[90] a new way of working, of speaking, of forming social relations among natural philosophers. This centered around the establishment of the experiment as a clearly defined and bounded way of life. Inside this realm defined by the experimental method, discussion was possible; but this made it unnecessary to decide the "metaphysical" questions of vacuum versus plenum.

Hobbes had many objections as a natural philosopher to the notion of a vacuum; what is of most interest here are the objections he had to the experimental community as politically dangerous. The key to this objection comes in the nature of the space that the experiment defines. As Shapin and Schaffer note, the public or private status of the experiment was a subject of intense debate in the seventeenth century. The very word "laboratory" carried with it secretist associations. By the last third of the century, in part because of the efforts of Boyle and the Royal Society, the laboratory had in effect become a kind of public space but with restricted access.[91]

The purely public quality of the experiment depended on what has been called "virtual witnessing." This is central to the scientific procedure and consists in the production in the mind of a reader of the image of an experiment. It requires "a technology of trust and assurance that the things had been done and done in a way claimed."[92] This cut at the very heart of the Hobbist enterprise. Communities, he knew, needed authority, or as he called it, masters. Masters were philosophers who had discovered fundamental matters; in practical terms, mastery was the Leviathan. The vision of the experimental community proposed by Boyle and the others was that of a society that was insulated and bounded from the community around it, thus avoiding the "civil wars" that wracked it. The purpose of this community was, among other things, to provide the kinds of goods that Restoration England required. It was another source of authority for all those, from brewers to theologians, who might benefit from "knowledge."

There was thus for Hobbes a kind of pretense in the claims of the Royal Society. On the one hand they claimed to be a community of free men, acting freely and without mastery; on the other, they provided knowledge to the structures of society. They made claim to the support of society (the Royal Society received a sizeable subvention), but claimed to be exempt from strictures of that society. If we bring this problem to the modern world we see immediately the parallels. Science is everywhere, yet unavailable to the public. It claims support from the public but refuses to be called into account. In any case, the public cannot call science to account for the public cannot understand it. This odd paradox of most open and most closed is clearly a problem as to the proper relation between science and politics.

To translate this analysis into terms made familiar by Kuhn, what Boyle and the others were asserting was that all science should be thought of as normal science, with clear-cut language boundaries. Hobbes understood that they were in fact doing much more than that and that the consequence of this practice of science being accepted as normal would affect other realms of society. He thus tried to portray their science as revolutionary, which would entitle him to a political defense.

Now when we looked at "revolutionary science," we saw that it tended to conceive of the facts themselves as problematic — what counted as a fact was the central question. Normal science, on the other hand, tends to think of problems as puzzles — a number of facts looking for a solution. The characteristic of normal science is that one tries to make the problematic, puzzling aspect of the subject matter go away; the characteristic of revolutionary science is that one tries to bring a problem into being. The two are structural inverses of each other.

Political theory consists of making the world problematic, of bringing new and different problems into existence. Note that I am not saying something as silly as racial discrimination was not a problem until it was noticed, brought into the public discourse. But I am saying that it was not a public, political problem until it was noticed by a certain number of people and in a certain way. This is the source of the relation of history to political science and political theory: it takes a certain number of people for something to be a problem, and that requires noise, fractiousness, a mess.

If, however, political science conceives of its activity as solving problems, it denies precisely the problem-making character of concern with the political. It becomes an attempt to dissolve the problematic, to solve the puzzle so that it is no longer a question.[93] In this sense, puzzles are the characteristic form of normal science — a discipline that constantly seeks to put its subject matter out of business. Speaking of revolutionary, non-normal science, Paul Feyerabend has remarked that, "science should not put an end to the very same questions to which it owes its existence."[94]

Then What Are We Doing Anyway?

I first argued that all activities including that of science are forms of communication and not reducible to single values. I further argued that it was incorrect to see the activity of the scientist as somehow resting on a "life-world" that was only approached hermeneutically. I then tried to relate to this a consideration of what it meant for something to have the status of a fact, and tried to show that "facts" do not correspond to any particular concept but are only facts with other facts, with which they form a loosely coherent world. I then argued that the particular form of communication that constituted the grammar of science was rationality. Rationality turned out on examination to be a multivoiced enterprise. I understood rationality as meaning, in part at least, "knowing what to do when" and found it based on a community of shared examples (experiences) which have been elaborated into some relationship with each other. In science, the values by which these examples are judged were accuracy, scope, simplicity, fruitfulness. These were not rules, and hence do not automatically prescribe behavior; they do form a community of intentions that define an activity as science and can modify over time.

I then suggested that to the degree that a community of investigators conceives of its task as puzzle oriented, rather than as problem raising, it will be generally self-destructive. There is nothing necessarily wrong with this: science is a kind of sequential forest-clearing.[95] To the degree, however, that political science is puzzle oriented, it denies, in a way that natural science does not, the nature of its own being. I would *not only* deny, then, that American political science has the paradigmatic nature sometimes attributed to it, but also that it can or should have such a nature.[96] If one were not to think that we *need* a paradigmatic quality, one would not make mistakes such as those made by Robert Dahl when he claimed in 1963 that "the full assimilation of Negroes into the normal system has already occurred in many Northern states."[97] Dahl here should not be seen in hindsight as a Ptolemaic astronomer about to be faced with a Copernican revolution. What proved Dahl conclusively short-sighted is a whole set of historical developments that had already started to emerge as problems in the late 1950s. Had Dahl been problem- rather than solution-oriented, he would have looked differently at what he took to be facts. (Another example of this can be seen in Dahl's later book, *Pluralist Democracy in the United States: Conflict and Consent,* in which he finds himself puzzled at the amount of violence in American history.)

Dahl, in other words, seems to have taken the facts for granted and to have reasoned in a manner something like this:

(1) Negroes were not integrated into the system when they were slaves. (Here both system and integration are left unproblematic.)

(2) Whites who were not slaves and not integrated into the system had a tendency towards violence (e.g., supposedly, late nineteenth-century Irish[98] — here the notion of violence is unexamined).

(3) As they became integrated into the system (an equation of integration with acquiring the vote — perhaps true in the case of the Irish but not necessarily true for all), they became peaceful (i.e., did not pose a public problem).

(4) In the North, negroes have the vote and are thus not kept out of the system, and hence do not pose a problem (meaning in 1963, we do not see a problem).

This sort of mistake comes from relying on your facts to make your system for you. It reflects what I am calling a puzzle attitude. Puzzles live and die by facts; problems make them.

What then might one say about political science as an activity? Along with Feyerabend, Lakatos, and Kuhn in the natural sciences, Henry Kariel[99] and J. G. A. Pocock[100] and others have argued for the view that political science should not be restricted by the notion that all has to proceed according to fixed rules and that it can be or should be more asking to play. "The idea," remarks Feyerabend, "that science can and should be run according to fixed rules and that its rationality consists in agreement with such rules, is both unrealistic and vicious."[101] Feyerabend and Kariel call for us to free ourselves from such imprisonment, often using metaphors drawn from the aesthetic realm in support of their position.

The image of play, perhaps even of "playing around,"[102] draws upon the classic function of the fool. In olden days, fools were hired not only to enliven court life by well-placed and slightly outrageous anecdotes and stunts, they also had certain privileges (of speech, for instance) and were occasionally mouthpieces for inconvenient yet accurate verities. (See *King Lear.*)

I have nothing against this notion of knowledge. But it should be noted that the existence of the fool depends on there being rules to be broken. When there is agreement in activity, when there are rules to be broken, the fool's stance is likely to be jarring and vital. A writer like Kariel presupposes this. But in a situation where there is not community, in which no rules are naturally authoritative, and thus no life is shared, only a set of procedures is tended and protected (this is what Weber calls *Fachmenschtum*), then the person playing the fool simply blows in the wind and is not heard. When such an act is played, professional fools disappear from the scene and serious madness may appear as the only path to redemption.[103]

All communities of discourse presuppose the same activities: the pleasures of agreement, the excitement of knowledge, the joys of discovery. They make possible the role of the fool who does not seem merely foolish, they give us rules to infringe, the chance to sin so that we may know better our humanity. These are what Calvin called the "posterior signs" of communities of activity. I have also indicated the tendency in the scientization of politics to make these communities of discourse impossible by putting an end to that which might bring us together.

Why should our profession do this? Bluntly, it may be that a community to which political theory would be available — as a community, in the manner I have described, not as a sack of potatoes — does not fully exist because, in some important sense, politics is not readily available. What might this mean? It obviously does not mean that people do not make decisions affecting each other's lives (although one might be hard put to say in this day of theatricality, that they govern). The tendency of political science to slide into sociology, economics, psychology, the transformation of political theory into theatricality and ethics may be a consequence of the fact that in the modern world politics is experienced as epiphenomenal.[104]

It is characteristic of modernity that each community of

discourse should call itself into question. Each activity is led by the nature of its investigations to pose questions which reflect the fact that we no longer know what to say about the world in some portions of our lives. At such times, the men and women who perform these activities are forced into self-examination. This is certainly painful, possibly productive. It may be that the reasons we will not come up with a general theory, a "paradigm," is that the world is not general for us — not now, but there is a time for everything, as Nietzsche knew. Thus, as in the past in religion and, Nietzsche tells us, in the future in morality, in politics we cannot now find anything real to share. But if we cannot now have a community of political discourse we must not then resolve that tension by transforming our politics into science, simply because *that* community is available. As we shall see in the next chapter, even Cassandra had her pleasures.

4. POLITICAL THEORY AND HISTORY: THE LURE OF THEORY

Deconstruction
D'ya wanta know the creed'a
Jacques Derrida?
dere ain't no reada
dere ain't no wrider
Eider.
　　　　　—Peter Mullen

I

IN 1953, T. D. Weldon published a short book entitled *The Vocabulary of Politics,*[1] which sought to bring the tools of "Oxford philosophy" to the terms of politics. The motivation behind this book was an anxiety that a great deal of metaphysical moss had grown up over the terms of politics, obscuring the obvious and the ordinary and leading to a series of questions that had no answers, to nonproblems. The book was an attempt to restore the ground to its "natural" state.

The book was in part a response to the sense that over the course of the early part of the twentieth century, theorists had developed a language that obscured, indeed, obfuscated, that which was clear. Political and moral confusions arose from what Hobbes might have called an insufficiency of speech.[2] What was uncontroversial and uncommented on about the book at the time was the striking claim that there was "the" vocabulary of politics. The presumption was that political theory was about a definable set of concepts, and its task was to refine this set well enough that the concepts fit with the facts

110

of the world. At that point we would have the last word, more or less, on these topics.

The desire to make transparent the relation between word and the world is a demand that the past not affect the present. It presumes that one can be in control of one's understanding such that the world will never betray itself as more than we understand it. This is what a theory aims for; this is the task of the theorist.

When Weldon wrote, the enthusiasm for what was understood as a new mode of philosophy was strong in the English-speaking world. He no doubt felt himself to be following the sense he gave to Wittgenstein's injunctions that philosophy aimed at "complete clarity," and that "if one tried to advance theses in philosophy, it would never be possible to debate them, because everyone would agree to them."[3]

I do not think that Weldon had Wittgenstein right. Wittgenstein's sentences do not tell us that our problem is simply to hack our way through metaphysical thickets until we reach the natural grass — a rather English lawn — but rather they suggest that philosophy does not properly proceed — do its work — by advancing *claims.* Wittgenstein argues that the task is to bring human beliefs into relief by confronting them with the agreements (forms of life) in terms of which those beliefs make sense.[4] But that Weldon misread Wittgenstein is revealing of a vision of the self as in control of the sense that he or she is making of the world. Why should one want "complete clarity"?

To follow this idea, we shall pursue the temptation to have the last word, to put an end to history — to find an answer to questions of political theory. What does it mean that we seek to come to conclusions, to a finality about the world?

Central to much contemporary political theorizing is the sense that it is natural or normal to seek final answers to moral and political problems. Liberal political theory draws most of its energy from the fact that such certainty has not been found. It is premised, in other words, upon the fact that human beings have not yet found the final answers, as if that were the underlying question and problem.

In this political theory betrays its ongoing debt to theology. There is in a good deal of contemporary political and ethical theory a sense of impending apocalypse. Take, for instance, Isaiah Berlin's classic essay, "Two Concepts of Liberty." Under the picture of negative and positive liberty lies a terrorized picture of what Berlin takes to be the modern world. Our lot, for Berlin, is constantly to confront diverging paths, choices that we make in a void.

> The world that we encounter in ordinary experience is one in which we are faced with choices between ends equally ultimate and claims equally absolute, the realization of some of which must inevitably involve the sacrifice of other.[5]

"In ordinary experience"! Indeed, we encounter this world, Berlin says, because all we have are "the ordinary resources of empirical observation and ordinary human knowledge." For Berlin, it is as if we are all Antigone, all the time. His is a picture of an individual whose experience gives him or her nothing to rely on, nothing of use in everyday life. For another instance, look at the work of John Rawls. In an article elaborating some of the claims he made in *A Theory of Justice*, Rawls writes:

> There are periods, sometimes long periods, in the history of any society during which certain fundamental questions give rise to sharp and divisive political controversy, and it seems difficult, if not impossible, to find any shared basis of political agreement. Indeed, certain questions may prove intractable and may never be fully settled. . . . There is no agreement on the way basic institutions of a constitutional democracy should be arranged.[6]

Confronted with this impossibility, Rawls begins his answer by proposing that we choose as if behind a "veil of ignorance."[7] There is much to be gained from this move, not the least of which is that it makes possible Rawls's demonstration that there is nothing that human beings naturally or historically *are* that is a good reason for giving one the right to dominate over another. But it is also true that behind the veil of ignorance is a state of terror. Rawls gives us a spectacle of a being absolutely naked and alone, knowing not who he is, what he can do, what he might be, whom he has been.[8] Rawls's rational chooser is a being in an extreme situation.[9]

Nor can this situation be resolved simply by asserting, as does, say, Robert Nozick, that human beings *have* certain qualities (are "rights-bearers").[10] The bald insistence that we are what we have relies too strongly on the metaphor of possession, precisely at the moment that possession should be questioned. What kind of being is capable of owning?

Something is wrong here. It is simply not the case that our ordinary experience, as Berlin has it, is *in extremis*. It becomes that way when we reflect on it — but this means that there is something wrong with our reflection. We need to examine what it would mean to make sense of the ordinary. What would a theory of the ordinary (not the extreme) be like? What kind of person would such a theorist be?

I wish to argue for the following ideas: One, that it is possible to write in a manner both meaningful and theoretical without insisting on either the last word or a disembodied self. This possibility corresponds to the particular manner in which human activity and historical conditions were related. Second, that most such contemporary writing implicitly rests on a notion of the person who might be in control of the world — this is what a theory is supposed to do, in this vision. We are, however, no longer able to operate successfully with this presupposition. Hence theory now will be something different than it had been before what Foucault has rather loosely called the "death of man."

I recognize that many readers will have decided from the preceding that it is all a matter of definition, that, "if that is what you want to call politics, well, then, of course. . . ." There is power to this objection, derived from the obvious fact that when Humpty Dumpty does fall off the wall, he does break and so does his world. Let me then spend a few paragraphs defending, in a manner at best only provocative or suggestive, the fact that I do not mean what I *want* to, but what I *have* to.

Some years ago the late Hannah Arendt suggested that this might not be the time to ask "who governs". Her reference was to the well-known book of Robert Dahl which had purported to discover those who "really" governed New Haven as opposed to those who "power" theorists like C. W. Mills claimed did. From Arendt's perspective, it was not really important whether Dahl or Mills were right; both of them shared a single perspective that there was someone who exercised functions which one might properly call those of governance. To such a claim she argued that modern man was subject not to governance, but to administration.[11] Her claim parallels that of Max Weber. He notes in *Economy and Society* that bureaucracy is the typical expression of the form of legitimacy in which obedience is due to and rests on norms rather than on persons.

> It is decisive for the specific nature of modern loyalty to office that, in the pure type, it does not establish a relation to a *person,* like the vassal's or disciple's faith in feudal or in patrimonial relations of authority. Modern loyalty is devoted to an impersonal functional [*sachlichen*] purpose.[12]

Bureaucracy has nothing to do with the truly political in Weber's analysis, for "politics means conflict" and thus "bureaucracy failed *completely* whenever it was expected to deal with political problems." Indeed, the "two forms are inherently alien" to each other.[13] This amounts to the claim that a certain experience of the world, namely, that part of politics which is concerned with governance (and one might add with citizenship, authority, and political community), has simply disappeared from human life (or, at least, is in the process of doing so).

Such a claim is often met with incredulity, and with the Lewis Carrollian assertion that "*we* don't mean by politics what the Greeks did," as if that were the end to it. Note the passage to the "we" from the accusatory "you" in "if that is what *you* want." Yet what do *we* mean then? And why should such a claim strike us as strange? Surely most people would agree that we simply no longer have the experience of kingship in the manner in which most people in the seventeenth century did. But that is an *aspect* of politics; doesn't the *category* remain?

This is a tricky matter and worth exploring for its byways. In the assertion "we don't mean by politics what the Greeks meant," there is a clear truth. Yet the desire that that be the end of the matter is an assertion that the "we" of the sentence is unproblematically related to what the Greeks (or anyone else) meant. It is an assertion that they are in no important way an Other for and with us. When linked to the Weldonian pursuit of "*the* vocabulary of politics" it is also an assertion of the epistemic priority of Weldon's limited "we" over any other. It is thus an assertion of the transcendental superiority of a particular "we" and the denial that it need be considered as an historical group in relation to other such groups.

This raises the general question of what it would mean to say that a theorist — say Plato, or Hobbes, or Rousseau — was wrong about something. I was once present at a lecture by the political theorist Allan Bloom at the end of which an ex-asperated philosopher remonstrated that "it was possible that Plato was wrong about *something*," as if that were obvious. I think at the time I wanted to agree, and if I did, I now think that I was wrong. It makes about as much sense to say that "Plato was wrong about something" as it does to say that "po-litical theory is wrong about something." The reason that "we don't mean by politics what the Greeks did" is necessarily be-side any interesting point is that we are not at liberty to change what a word means. Those words form the texts which are the manifestations of our ability to make sense of the world in which we live. While it is always true that the world is richer than any text we have of it, it is also true that we make sense of it only as a text. (This is another way of reading Kuhn's paradigms and Foucault's *epistèmes*.) Hence, if a text is to be a text of political theory, it will be part of a community of discourse that will include other texts of political theory.

However, there is no world-historical necessity that there be a community of discourse of political theory. If it makes any sense to say that "Philosophy started with the Greeks," or to suggest with Stephen Toulmin and June Goodfield that the theoretical attitude was unknown to the Babylonians,[14] or that "Socrates was the founder of political philosophy"—then it also makes sense to say that an activity that has come into history can also leave it.

We are forced then to raise the question of the consequences of the fact that our various modes of discourse—among them, politics and religion—are themselves historical. That is, they came into being at different times and constitute no more naturally necessary ways of organizing a world than did, say, alchemy. Note that I am not raising the question of the "truth" of these statements. I am only saying that there is no necessity that people organize their world politically, nor that they engage (tacitly or explicitly) in political theory. If we are to understand what it means to claim to see the world politically, then we must have as part of that understanding that it is not naturally required of us.

Take religion as another example. Many of us can say that we have tacitly recognized what Nietzsche was perhaps the first to see, that religion is increasingly no longer available to us, that we have become in Max Weber's happy phrase, "religiously unmusical." Whatever one wants to mean by "religion," it seems wrong to speak of what many of us experience religiously as the same sort of thing that men and women experienced 300 years ago in Massachusetts Bay. If there is anything that the existentialist movement and the experience of the insanity of the first fifty (eighty?) years of the twentieth century might have imprinted in us, it is this realization. And if in religion, then why not in politics, and perhaps in the future in morality? Nietzsche was suggesting nothing else. To investigate such thoughts it is necessary to go back to those periods where one might want to claim that theoretical writing was possible and the experience of politics was available to men.[15] I propose here to return to a brief consideration of the kind of writing which, one would *have to* admit, has been involved in important political perceptions of the world and which has made a difference, or has been connected with those times when a difference was made.

I should make a couple of disclaimers here. I have the greatest respect for the importance and validity of careful examination and exegesis of the great writers of the traditions, for the difficulty of doing that well and accurately and for the learning and effort which such an enterprise requires. I do not want to address the question of precisely what the nature of that importance is—it can be seen from the claims I make in writing this essay that I think that the importance cannot be collective, but probably only individual.[16] In any case, properly speaking, this essay is not about theorists: I am not attempting an exegesis of Rousseau or Hobbes in order to explain why they are "relevant" to our age. Such attempts, often combined with descriptions of why Aristotle resembles some modern political sociologist, seem to me inherently retrograde, and respondent to the attempt to find some sort of rationalized intellectual ancestry. I am claiming explicitly what I have been practicing in the first three chapters, namely that the texts of political theory are as present in our world as *we* make them.[17] This depends on the readers, not on the texts.

One should ask what makes theoretical writing "work," when it does? The answer to this is controversial and tortuous, but involves the following sort of things (and here some of the topics we have seen in the last two chapters become useful).

One of the things we saw in the last chapter was that knowledge does not move only by a better and better description of facts.[18] The concentration on facts can only be a pre- or non-theoretical attitude. One of the contributions of the new "anthropology of science," as Bruno Latour has named it, is to show that no one can find their theory lying about in the realm they are investigating. To say this, however, does not make clear what the source of theory is. If it is not to be found, then clearly it must be deduced or made.

Why can it not be *found?* It is not in *nature* like an item anymore than the plot is *in* a novel. Theory is a manner of making sense out of experiences which are considered "information." In this we are forced to realize that theorizing is an act different from simply putting facts side by side, as if to build a house simply by laying bricks. Were one to restrict oneself to the facts, one would have to assert a principle of "association by continuity,"[19] which is to say that one approached facts as if simply trying to figure out how they fit together.

We know from work done in epistemology and psychology that there is no predetermined manner in which facts "naturally" fit together.[20] The world does not make itself available to us as motley or completely disparate facts: most of the time — to the surprise of my adolescent son — we do make sense to each other.

Why so? There is no way that we can experience the world except as known. It is in the nature of the world as present to humans to be known.[21] I do not want to claim that order is "created" by the knower, but rather to assert that as the world makes us so we make the world. This is what Nietzsche meant by referring to knowledge as a form of the will to power.

The sense which objects make in the world(s) available to us is not immediately apparent to us, for the structures which hold the world together are not apparent, but can be made so. Merleau-Ponty once noted that "one must *awaken* the perspectival experience";[22] that sense must be *aroused* ("provoked" is the word I took from Emerson) is an indication that what makes something what it is, that facticity itself, is the necessary preliminary question of theory.

If the above is sensible, theory must deal with the question of what makes something what it is, accepting the fact that it is never particularly clear (that is, clear only as a particular) *what* something is. To find out what something "is," then, is to examine the relation between ourselves and that which we look at, and at the same time the relations between that

relationship and the relations of that which we look at. We
are then as theoretical actors forced to deal with a whole world
and with our experience *in* it (Merleau-Ponty says, "We choose
our world and the world chooses us").[23]

If this is so, then we need not be really interested in the
"truth" of a political theory. I want to make my own a distinction between the "truth" of a claim and its "truthfulness."[24] It
is clear that there are certain claims about the world that are
(or are not) true. "Mont Blanc is 4807 meters high" is such
a claim, and is true (I looked it up). One need not entertain
surrealist notions such as "it depends what you mean by a
meter" or "how do you know?" Whatever it means for something to be true, it means something like this kind of statement.

It is a different matter when one approaches the kinds of
statements about the world made in political theory. I have
resisted—and shall further resist in chapter five—the tendency
to call the claims of political theory "normative." (I have also
not said that they are not.) Above I suggested that it was not
very interesting to be concerned with whether or not "Locke
was right about property." I would call the kind of statement
made by political theory "truthful." By that I mean that I must
accept it, find myself in it. It is true that there is no (external)
necessity that I find myself in it—nor can I compel you to acknowledge its truthfulness—to find yourself in it. (I could compel you, with the satisfying passive aggressivity of pointing
to an encyclopedia, to admit to the height of Mont Blanc.)
Not everyone is capable of responding to political theory; perhaps it is the case that not everyone is capable of responding
to the political life. The claim that life is under certain conditions "solitary, poor, nasty, brutish and short" is not meant
to be true (or false); it is meant to strike us, for us to find it
in ourselves, perhaps even in our rejection of it. It is this quality that makes it truthful.

Note also that truths are more subject to history than is
the truthful. Much of what Robert Dahl wrote in *Who Governs?* was true at the time he wrote it. Little of it is now. The
truthful, on the other hand, retains it capacity to strike hu-

mans at all points. Indeed, there is much to be learned from understanding why it is that people are struck by a given thought, now, and in these times. (The current rage for Hobbes and the ascendance of rational choice theory have something to do with each other and say something about our world in the English-speaking West in the late 1980s.)

In this the truthfulness of political theory is the kind of authority and community of discourse which we looked at in the first chapter. If I say that truthfulness comes when I must acknowledge a claim as mine, I mean that I could not deny it and still be myself. (As Prospero comes finally to recognize about Caliban: "This thing of darkness, I acknowledge mine.") Political theory is texts that draw from us the admission that how it is with me, it is also with you, even though you are not my friend, or my lover, or my parent, or in contract with me. The authority of the text comes from the fact that it provokes *us*.

These preliminary realizations permit a certain amount of ground clearing which seems essential if we are to make any progress in understanding the nature of theory. They will also help us to distinguish theory from ideology. We are not here in the world of ultimate choices that Berlin or Rawls give us, nor yet in that of the enforced nature on which Robert Nozick insists.

* * *

All social sciences, but perhaps most sharply political science, are both witness to and battleground for a debate between those who claim to be theoretically oriented and those who are trying to deal with the "real" world. Traditionally this argument turned around the "fact-value" debate. Let us approach this problem from the vantage point we have now reached.

Proponents of dealing with the world "as it is" have deplored as nonsensical the attempts to find out how the world *should* be from an examination of the facts of the world. Facts simply *are* and to pretend that they force us to like them or not is simply metaphysical garbage. While it is now somewhat fashionable to discount this positivist position, it should be noted that those men and women we identify as "logical positivists" had an almost Promethean urge to cleanse the philosophical world of extraneous baggage they thought had accumulated over the centuries and to *see* simply and clearly. Perhaps Prometheus was confused with Hercules: that the task was more complicated than men like Ayer and Schlick and Neurath realized need not prevent us from remembering the central thrust of their endeavor. Seeing clearly is a theoretical motivation.

Those offended by the radical division of the world into two parts, the one dealing with values, the other with facts, responded in a number of ways. One typical response was to demonstrate (or purport to) that the separation was impossible and that all statements about the world are enmeshed in an interaction that includes humans and therefore by definition responds to "values." There is obvious truth to this objection, not the least of which is derived from its opposing the enterprise of separating people off from their life. The objection remains problematic, however, insofar as it persists in attaching values only to human beings. The model which this objection adopts is premised on the notion that values are "human stuff" and are what we bring *to* the world; such a distinction derives from the very premise on which the critique is based, namely, the inseparability of these two worlds.[25]

Though it is fairly clear that the rigid separation of facts and values is untenable from a conceptual point of view, the accusations that positivists are themselves equally "value laden" is not particularly telling. And if the claim is that they are biased in a self-serving way, the claim is either untrue or trivial.

This debate is in the end sterile, for, at best it can only result in the proponents of the fact-value division recognizing their own attachment to society. We do not gain *any* theoretical knowledge or ability and remain only on the surface of investigation. We have still not found out *what* makes particular facts make sense, and we can only surmise the statistical likelihood of certain phenomena seeming to fit together.

The theoretical enterprise is different from the empirical one. It does not consist of finding new information, but in seeing what information we have in a theoretical manner, in trying to figure out what makes information make sense to us, or more properly exactly what makes it information to us at all. This is perhaps most true or most obvious in the social sciences, but also true in the natural sciences. Regularities are observed there, perhaps predictions even made on the basis of sufficient observation. However we would not properly speak of such activity, even if of Babylonic complexity, as theoretical. It remains, in Raymond Aron's words, "too close to empirical reality."[26]

True knowledge, even prediction, is not then inherently theoretical and there is no reason to assume that it will lead to theory.[27] What we want to know is, in Thoreau's words, "precisely why these objects compose a world," with every word in that query stressed. This is the reason that the fact-value distinction proves of little or no use in the writing of theory. What we are after is a manner of seeing the world such that its sense is laid transparently bare to us. *We* (the we in the previous sentence) are beings who have a particular historical and social position. Hence our seeing clearly, while not dependent on a particular position in the world, will be revelatory of something about ourselves.

This is a problematic point, but a good understanding of it reveals why the theoretical act must be grasped in terms of the change it makes in those to whom it is available. Properly understood, the theorist is not one who imposes his or her order on the world, but rather one who makes available the particular limitations of different ways of being in the world. Thus there is an inherent contradiction in the theoretical act. The more completely one makes oneself available to the world, the more that self is in danger of dissolving. Nietzsche notes in *Beyond Good and Evil:*

> It might be a basic character of existence that those who would know it completely would perish, in which case the strength of spirit should be measured according to how much

"truth" one could still barely endure — to put it more clearly, to what degree one would *require* that it be thinned down, shrouded, sweetened, blinded, falsified.[28]

I am asserting here that to do theory is to be changed and that one cannot do theory without change happening. The beginnings of this position were laid out in an article by Charles Taylor, "Neutrality in Political Science," and more recently by W. Connolly, in *Appearance and Reality in Politics*.[29] Taylor argued that while facts do not *lead* to theory, they make a difference to theory, and in fact affect the development of theory. Hence facts are not theory neutral in political science any more than they were in the natural world.

This, however, does not make them "values." Taylor tends to remain within the notion of facts and values in that he thinks that theory is not "neutral" from a value point of view. Had he pushed his analysis beyond this he would have seen that although he had shown that facts affect theory, he had not accounted for there being facts at all nor why *these* facts are the ones presented to us. Merleau-Ponty, whose writings on perception have been the most successful attempt so far as the beginning of a resolution of this problem, once noted that "nothing is more difficult than to know exactly just what we do see."[30] The problem is not as some have claimed[31] that "what we see depends on where we sit"; to hold that position would be to reduce all of science to more or less self-conscious ideology. The position is true, but for our purposes quite uninteresting. To see clearly will be to learn something of where one is sitting, for it is especially one's *position* that is not obvious here.

The act of coming to find out why the facts that we observe make sense *must require that we give ourselves an account of our own position in the world which is part of these facts*. This was Weber's position at the beginning of the *Religionssoziologie*, when he suggests that "any product of Western civilization must ask himself how it is that in the West and in the West only" structures of rationalization have grown up.[32] The giving of an account is not more important in this requirement than

the fact that we "must" give it. It is demanded of us if we are
to be ourselves, and it establishes us with others. One can see
a parallel sense of the demands of the truthful in Nietzsche's
account of the impetus behind the writing of the *Birth of Tragedy*. Throughout the book the rhetoric is that of compulsion
and the author appears almost passive in the face of the demands of his subject. "We had to emphasize an Apollonian
illusion . . . We thought we had observed . . . ; We were forced
to recognize . . . ; The revelation seems to summon us." All
of these examples are from the first two pages of chapter twenty-
four and it would not be difficult to do the same for other
chapters.[33] On another level, in Beckett's *Endgame*, the dialogue appears as absurd or nonsequitur gibberish until we understand that Beckett has reproduced the sounds and the patterns (and the sense) of our everyday language. We come to
hear ourselves and attain with that an insight into the terrors
and hopes of being human in the everyday world.[34] In the political world, Marx claimed, our insight into what makes up
the world of capitalism will change our position in relation
to it.[35]

What is the source of this dynamism? The answer to this
question is complicated. It will have different sources in different fields and areas of inquiry. The accounts which Newton, or Heisenberg, or Einstein have given of the effect of their
theoretical insights on themselves have been concerned with
new appreciations of the nature of the mind, with Kantian
questions, one might almost say.[36] One could argue that the
nature of the theoretical act in natural sciences draws its power
from the experiences of the relation of the human mind to
that which the mind must admit surpasses it. With politics
and society, there is probably (another) source of power, the
making available of possible and new relationships between
human beings and the patterns of change which are taking
place in the society to which the theorist is addressed. This
might be thought of as an extension of the person in time and
space. It is at this point that Kuhn's concept of normal science
may help us.

II

I should like to derive the notion of normal politics from the parallel notion of normal science used by Kuhn in his *The Structure of Scientific Revolutions*. He developed there a model of science as oscillating between periods of normalcy and revolutions which mark the introduction of new paradigms of thought. Most of the furor which greeted his work focused around the notion of revolution — those conceptual breaks in thought which mark the movement from one manner of seeing the world to another. As important, however, as the concept of revolution is that of normal science. (Kuhn even gives some indications of this in his pained response to J. W. Watkins's sour attack in *Criticism and the Growth of Knowledge*.[37]) This is "ordinary science," the kind that most of us expect to happen most of the time and result in discoveries of greater or lesser interest and use. The very familiarity we have with "normal science" should lead us to examine it more closely, for it is, indeed, wonderful. How is it that a particular sphere of endeavor can yield such results and in a manner that the human beings engaged in it can expect it to?[28] What precisely does the term "normal" mean when applied to humans?

Briefly, I would propose something like this. An activity can be considered normal when, generally speaking, those engaged in it know what to do when confronted with a situation which demands action and can have a reasonable expectation that their action will lead to results not too dissimilar to those which they expect. In such situations, having a science means that one expects the world to make sense. The elements of the science are not or need not each time be articulated: they are part of and define the activity of doing whatever one does. The activity in question may be considered normal because one does it without thinking (in the way that we do not think *about* the rules of chess once we know how to play) and without problem. One knows, to use Wittgenstein's happy phrase about the resolution of philosophical problems, "one's way about."

With this in mind we might then say that a theorist is the person who gives a formulation of general changes which are happening to the society and to the people in it in such a manner that a new and, for those making it, "better" coherence is available. Typically this has happened with those men whom we now view as forming the tradition of Western political thought. One might instance the change from the understanding of the world in terms of family (James I) to that in terms of body (Hobbes).[39] There are other equally striking examples. Jean Pierre Vernant, for instance, has argued that Hesiod and Homer give particular definition to person and time, a definition not in itself necessary, but in itself possible given the general nature of the Ionian world, and central to our later understanding of personhood.[40]

In all of these cases, the *power* of theory gives it "truthfulness," not "truth." It is the capacity of the theoretical act to call out, to provoke, that determines its truthfulness. Max Weber writes:

> There is one standard: that of success in the recognition of concrete cultural phenomenon in their interdependence, the causal determination and their significance.[41]

From this, two important principles follow: first, that any definition given in the movement from one state of normal politics to another, while shaped by the logic of the movement, is a change *not* completely defined by external circumstances. A *number* of resolutions are possible. We might call revolutions "underdetermined" and adopt a stance in criticism of positions such as that of Louis Althusser, who claims that revolutionary change occurs only at periods of "overdetermination." A situation is "overdetermined" when all the structural vectors of society come together at one point and produce a particular and predicted effect. In practice, Althusser's position amounts to asserting that such changes do not result from human action. It eliminates the role of the political.[42] For there to be a conception of politics, a number of resolutions must be thought possible, not all of which will be equally effective —

finding that out is what the tragedies and triumphs of world history are made of.

Second, and this point follows from the first, whatever resolution is attained will of necessity be *a* particular resolution — that is, it will have a *particular* historical contingency and will thus be subject to change over time. Our world is made out of particular resolutions, not the attainment of a complete pattern. It is for this reason I have been asserting that the world is always more than we can make of it, but that anything we make of it has the status of a text.[43]

I have suggested that the successful text changes not only the world which it formulates, but also necessarily changes the theorist. All political theory is, we might say, maculate, in that the author of the text does not escape from the analysis that he proposes for us. This gives theory a kind of uncontrolled quality: therefore it is not surprising that those who would be theorists have often, most often, tried to remain above and escape the world of their making. In practice, this consists in claiming that one's own theory is true; in criticism, it consists in claiming that another's theory is "merely the expression of his (or her) values." In other words, it claims at least the possibility of a transcendental position for one's self and the irreducible earth-bound character of an opponent. Against this, the claim of truthfulness, with the dynamics which we have seen as part of it, denies both the claim to transcendance, and the counter-claim of ideology. Truthfulness cannot be proved: it simply has to be there.[44] We have dealt in previous chapters with the temptations of theatricalization and science; here I see two additional general manners in which theorists have tried to avoid being marked by the terms they offer the world.

The first general category can loosely be called the functionalist response — the notion that all societies must perform certain universal tasks or functions in order to remain in existence. This idea is generally tied to the belief that societies "want" to remain in existence. The most standard criticism of functionalist approaches is that they are unable to account for change. Such attacks typically come from those with a more dynamic or developmental vision of the historical process.

There is some truth to this accusation, though not the one most critics want to make. For functionalists, there is no necessary relation between the theoretical act and the production of change. The functions that a society "must" perform are the categories through which the functionalist seeks to make sense of the world. They are thus categories *of* the world. It would follow from this that the production of change in the world is in no way related to the act of understanding. It presumes an immaculate notion of theory, producing no change either in the world or in the theorist and his or her audience. It neatly delineates what would count as intervention and leaves that choice up to the social scientist who might want to turn activist.[45]

Functionalism remains unself-conscious about the dynamic inherent in its categories, and becomes in practice culturally bound. Edmund Leach delightfully chronicled the confusions of the British Colonial office when it sought the leadership structures of Kachin Burmese tribes.[46] That "leaders" should have been, in proper English tradition, those through whom taxes were collected proved simply meaningless in the Kachin context. This notion of leadership in no way made sense of elements of the Kachin society at that time. It resonated in nothing and responded to nothing. Theoretical concepts, contrary to the unspoken presumptions of functionalist thinking, do not function as generally appropriate tools devoid of specific context or historical references which can be passed from scientist to scientist like a hammer.

In addition, the notion that it is "society" which "performs" functions should give us pause. What and where is the society which performs these functions? It can only be seen as coterminous with these functions. If this is not admitted, then what the functionalist must do is reify the notion of society. It becomes a "thing" which "does" certain acts. Here the same mistake is committed as with facts in the case of the empiricist. There is a presumption that the fact can be separated from that which makes it a fact (i.e., from a specific historical situation or pattern) and here is the presumption that functions can be separated from the specific society which "performs" them.

Thus the functionalist perspective must remain only that, a perspective which reflects only the surface of the phenomenon and is kept from discovering what makes the particular matters investigated make sense to us. There does not seem to be anything particularly *wrong* with this. A great deal of useful and interesting information can be found out by such enterprise. I am only concerned here that such an approach can neither lead to theory, nor is it theory in itself. It may be as complex and useful as Babylonian astronomy, but it remains fundamentally *useful* knowledge and not constitutive, not theory.

The second perspective which constitutes a response to the problem of making sense of society can be labeled as the structural phenomenological. Here the theorist can be totally melded with the subject. This perspective has its origins perhaps in an aspect of the thought of Max Weber, whose anguished separation of fact and value was the basis not of the assertion of the possibility of science, but of the impossibility of finding a point where one might stand and be both theoretically significant and politically relevant.

Such a divorce between the stance of the theorist and his life in the world has continued to affect theorists in one manner or another since Weber's time. The conclusion to Lévi-Strauss's *Tristes Tropiques* — a now too often ignored book which remains seminal to an account of this century — is an express withdrawal of both word and deed from the possibilities of activism in theory. Lévi-Strauss proclaims that the scientist must

> accept the mutilated condition which is the price of his vocation. He has chosen and must accept the consequences of his choice. His place lies with the others and his role is to understand them. Never can he act in their name, for their very otherness prevents him from thinking or willing in

their place: to do so would be tantamount to identifying himself with them. He must also resign himself to taking no action in his own society for fear of adopting a partisan position . . . ; his initial choice will remain and he will make no attempt to justify that choice. It is a pure motiveless act.[47]

It is quite wrong to identify this text as simply an advocacy of value-free anthropology. The argument is a theoretical and moral one, directed in part against Sartre and possibly Merleau-Ponty,[48] and premised on the understanding that an activism in word or deed will necessarily lead to partisanship. One should note that Lévi-Strauss's response is that this is true of certain *types* of writing and that the problem is to find a form of writing which does not take a position, which does not change the writer and that about which he writes. Even in public ceremonies, Lévi-Strauss follows this principle. The beginning of his inaugural address at the Collège de France forms an annihilation of any significance which might attach to the fact of *his* assumption of the Chair of Social Anthropology.[49] He begins by placing himself in a numerological mythology of social anthropology, extends the principle of the number governing the myth to the natural world, both animate and inanimate, such that within two pages of text he has simply abstracted the historical and temporal significance from the activity being performed.

What Lévi-Strauss does is to make himself into a text, that is, deny the necessary incompleteness of his relation to that which he has written, the necessary disjuncture between the world and our way of being in it. To the degree that this can be realized — it is in literature, see Proust — such activity is both honest and to a great degree successful. It is honest in that it recognizes the relation between the sort of statement that a theorist must make and the society with which he is dealing. It is no accident that the choice of partisanship or complete identification is the most strongly posed in those structural and phenomenological sciences that deal with societies which are dominated by the synchronic and not the diachronic. Properly speaking, synchronic societies or systems do not de-

velop — they remain always the "same," in the way a kaleido-
scope does, adopting different and more or less complex formulations of the same structures. There cannot be a question
of having to make sense of them in the manner by which theorists have had to in the past in the more diachronic societies.
If there is no developing principle, then, by virtue of what
I argued before, namely, that political theory works through
a power drawn from the (successful) presentation of a formulation of dynamics inherent in the change of society, there can
be no political theory in a society which is predominantly synchronic in nature. The most striking thing about writers like
Lévi-Strauss is how willingly he accepts, indeed welcomes,
the fact that political theory is impossible; one suspects, since
he intends *his* as a general account of the world, that he holds
it true not only for those tribes of the *pensée sauvage* which he
has investigated but increasingly for all societies. Lévi-Strauss
has countered the dangers of ideology by inventing a world
in which ideology cannot exist. As Bruno Latour has written:
"Lévi-Strauss finds no other solution but to transform the savage mind into an *alter ego* of the scientific one. . . . The two
have to be similiar — so as to avoid the discriminatory bias,
while remaining infinitely distant — to avoid pollution."[50]

The end of *The Scope of Anthropology* gives to his audience,
in terms as moving as they are unpolitical, the dangers and
the promise of diachrony:

> After rendering homage to the masters of social anthropol-
> ogy at the beginning of this lecture, let me devote my last
> words to those 'primitives' whose modest tenacity still offers
> us a means of assigning to human facts their true dimen-
> sions. Men and women who, as I speak, thousands of miles
> from here on some savannah ravaged by brush fire, or in
> some forest under torrential rain, are returning to camp
> to share a meagre pittance and to invoke their gods together;
> those Indians of the tropics and their counterparts through-
> out the world who have taught me their humble knowledge
> (in which is contained, nevertheless, the essence of the
> knowledge which my colleagues have charged me to trans-

mit to others): soon, alas, they are all destined for extinction under the impact of illnesses and — for them even more horrible — modes of life with which we have plagued them. To them I have incurred a debt which I can never repay, even if, in the place in which you have put me, I were able to give some proof of the tenderness which they inspire in me and of the gratitude which I feel towards them by continuing to be as I was among them, and as, among you, I would hope never to cease from being: their pupil, their witness.[51]

For Lévi-Strauss, outside reference points are dangerous and to be avoided. Were this to be true and necessary of our world, or were our world to become such that reference points no longer existed, then by definition political theory such as we have known it would be impossible.

III

Yet at some level all of this must ring as incorrect. There has been such a thing as political theory; it has affected the way people thought and acted; it has had the activist quality which I have attributed to it. Most simply we know that people wrote, others listened and read and found a self in those sentences and books, some formulation which led them to perceive and act differently than they might otherwise have. Perhaps those who read Hobbes did not act as Hobbes might have hoped that they would; but that is Hobbes, the man, and not Hobbes, the author. It is in any case likely that they did not act as if divine right were the only source of legitimation for government.[52] For there to be a complete unity between words and the world would deny the very stuff of humanity.

Thus Tocqueville reports in the *European Revolution* that at first "Montesquieu was cited, but at the end no one but Rousseau was." Similarly, Norman Jacobson has suggested that American political science might have turned out quite differently if "instead of the prudence of James Madison, the pieties

of Thomas Paine had become the chief text for political education in America."[53] The argument need not be that political
theorists *caused* a revolution, but only that their formulation
provided a possible activity program for those who heard and
assimilated it.[54]

We are forced to ask then why theory worked in the past,
how precisely these conceptual revolutions, or "recontextual-
izations" to use Kuhn's later phrase, came about. The particular power of political theory came from its attachment to a
process of change which was taking place without the complete volitional control of human beings. In such a situation
there is not a complete unity between intention and result.
What is involved here, Hegel remarks in the *Philosophy of History*,

> is that something else results from the actions of men than
> that which they intend and achieve, something else than
> that they know and want. They accomplish their interest;
> but something else is accomplished, which was implied in
> it, but which was not in the consciousness and the inten-
> tions of the actors.[55]

It is precisely this disjuncture which makes political theory
possible; which allows men and women to provoke and be provoked and to constitute a community of authority and intentions. The power of theory was a power leached from the dynamism of history and that dynamism in turn implied that
the activity and intentions of humans carried with them implications which would be worked out. It is the working out
of that disjuncture, of a particular manner of thinking of the
world, which forms the channel in which the waters of a particular politics may flow. What is wrong with the functionalists and phenomenologists is that they seek to stand above it.

Political theory is a way of overcoming the problem of time
and the past. It presupposes that the past is a force which affects humans both consciously and not, and that men and
women find in each other the understanding and acceptance
of, not to say the ease with, a certain portion of their life. It
is specifically concerned with our ability to come to grips with

what happens to us when we live in communities which change in ways that occasionally surprise us, but to which we still feel bound. The existence of life together — the consequence of Epimetheus' forgetfulness — is after all what makes politics possible. Socrates in the *Phaedrus* and the *Apology* proclaims his attachment to the city, for it is only there that he can learn of himself and others.

That today we might think that the actual quality of completely human relations was better understood by Rousseau, Marx, and Durkheim than by Hobbes, Locke, and Mill in no way controverts the common claim that the relation of persons to persons has formed the theoretical and practical core of the political world.

IV

What in modern Western society affects the possibility of theory? Recent times have seen much discussion of what it is fashionable to refer to as the "post-industrial society." Much — certainly too much — has been included under this term. Yet central to all usages is the notion that the social fabric is in the process of changing, that men and women are not held together by the necessity and importance of common pursuits.[56]

This occurrence has been analyzed on two levels, one the structural, and the other, the psychosocial. On the structural level, John Schaar has argued that in the case of "legitimacy," that is, the consequence of the actuality of authority which makes common life possible in politics, legitimacy, properly understood, rests on "an element of law or right (which) . . . rests on foundations external to and independent of the mere assertion or opinion of the claimant. . . ." One can find, he goes on to note, a variety of such sources, "immemorial custom, divine law, the law of nature, a constitution." Schaar then demonstrates that the development of the modern bureaucratic state is such that "men have determined to live without collective ideals and disciplines, and thus without obedience to and reliance on the authorities that embody, defend and replenish those ideals." The system works, he continues, "not because recognizable human authority is in charge, but because its basic ends and procedural assumptions are taken for granted and programmed into men and machines."[57]

Schaar is arguing that the nature of the modern state is to make human collective activity not so much impossible as unnecessary. For him the quality of human relations changes in modern society in a manner such that whole realms of behavior which were once important to human beings now disappear and are not *replaced*. It is important to escape the functionalist and structuralist trap of arguing that "political functions" are replaced by other functions. Such a notion presupposes ultimately that the fabric of human experience simply does not and will not vary.[58] As noted before, Hannah Arendt once argued that the contemporary experience of politics is very different from that of the Greeks, but what is often missed in her analysis is the claim that human experience is thereby *lessened*. The availability of public discourse is less than it was one hundred and forty years ago. In religion, *nothing* has really replaced the world which was God's, even if we continue to act as if something could. "We live," Max Weber wrote with a sense of loss, "as did the olden world, not yet disenchanted of its gods and demons, but in another sense: just as the Hellene at times sacrificed to Aphrodite and then to Apollo and before all to the Gods of his city, so do we still, but disenchanted and disrobed of the mythic but inward true plasticity of that stance."[59]

In his "Radical Politics and the Welfare State,"[60] Michael Walzer seeks to investigate the particular sources of this altered quality of relationships. He finds that the increasing ability of the state to deliver the goods to most if not all members of the state makes the state "more powerful and its members thus more dependent on its benevolence." The result is not that the individual is subjected to tyranny—far from it. Rather the interaction of people to get something for themselves collectively tends to fall away.

Specifically, Walzer finds that large numbers of people realize for the first time that the state *should* be doing something for them. The attitude that one has the right to expect that the state will help each person leads to the realization that the state is neither mystical nor endowed with an impervious legitimacy; rather it leads to a new and rationalistic legitimacy in which demands are universalized to all individuals. Since each person feels that he has a right to individual benefits from the state, it is much less important for people to know each other in terms of political organization. (After all, Lenin did not think that the Czar had an *obligation* to benefit the workers — had he so thought there would have been no revolution.) The state thus becomes both in fact and in spirit an administrative agency, and the possibility of the attachment of the individual to some sort of collective value is greatly diminished.

In more direct language, developments in the modern state tend to make the collective relation — the "we" — among people unnecessary. And we find quite naturally that the logical end of this process is the absence of an effective public world. As Otto Kirchheimer wisely noted:

> The privacy of mass civilization is at the same time privacy and protection against mass civilization. . . . Mass man's withdrawal is not regulated by self-confidence and coolness towards those agencies which would guide his consumer and leisure time satisfaction. The reason is that these agencies are insufficiently related to the major problem of his existence: his purpose in life.[61]

Kirchheimer's analysis points to the conclusion that the structure of modern society is such that the public world no longer provides an effective arena for having a life and that thus one looks elsewhere. This does not mean that the same kind of life can be found elsewhere: it will be a different life.

This recognition is the basis of the second sort of analysis of post-industrial society, an analysis which we might call "psycho-social." The following analysis really describes at the individual level what the first analysis described at the structural and social level. Whether the second sort of analysis focuses on individual cases[62] or on societies,[63] the language is fundamentally individual and psychological in nature. The quality of such an approach strikes me as very uneven and most often suffers from an attempt to come up with *the* reason why things are changing.

The unspoken but central assumption is the proposition that middle-class values have a certain psychological coherence for all income levels. This coherence is structured around a particular "reality principle," namely, groups whose founding principle was essentially economic in nature. By claiming that the central collective reality of such groups is economic, I mean to say that it is based on the ability to defer gratification when it can be seen that quantitatively greater gratification can possibly be achieved in the future should immediate gratification be deferred. This presumes a world which we see or imagine not as scarce in resources, but as requiring only restraint to make those resources even greater. The politics of such a world rests on an economic way of doing things: it is here that Marx saw the most deeply (*our* politics are increasingly epiphenomenal to our economics) and erred the most extensively (not *all* politics have been so nor need they be). But Faust's bargain was for all acquisition, until he said "verweil doch."

The psychological coherence of bourgeois society (as I will call it for convenience) thus depends on the continued perception of the reasonableness of deferring gratification. In our times, two sorts of things seem to be happening simultaneously. Whether they will cancel each other out or not remains to be seen. On the one hand many younger people no longer expect that the deferring of gratification will lead to greater rewards in the future. Furthermore they expect (given the welfare state) that they will be or can be taken care of on at least a minimal level. If the deferring of gratification no longer leads to anything quantitatively more satisfying than nondeferring, it is reasonable to refuse the reality principle of the society.

Reactions here can be as various as they were in the 1960s: withdrawal, pretense, the creation of a new and more demanding reality principle, often extra- or anti-legal.

The second development comes in situations where the economic achievement is quantitatively sufficient to satisfy. We know from the work of Herbert Simon that organizations often tend to "satisfice" — that is, to work to get past a threshold of acceptability and not on an uninterrupted linear scale — rather than to maximize (e.g.) profits. So also perhaps with individuals, in which case there would be a threshold effect, a quantitative level after which the reality principle would simply not work. In a society which, due to its economic basis, must be deficient in solidary incentives (having a surplus of individual purpose norms), human beings in this situation must move in a direction of normlessness. After a certain point, one would say, they do not know with whom they stand and live, for their reality principle only governs a limited portion of their life.

Both of these analyses strike me as essentially similar, and different only in their scope. They both argue that reality principles are historically limited in scope or effectiveness. For the first, the vacuum of normality pervades much of life. For the second, only a portion. (This was perhaps most strongly seen in a CBS special called "What if the Dream Came True?" where a high-level bank executive, having risen from the ranks and reached success in early middle age, realized that he did not know why he did what he did, but was unable to make the leap to questioning whether or not he *should* be doing what he did.) In both of these cases there are a number of consequences following from the collapse of a reality principle adequate to generate common behavior appropriate to and satisfying of the situation. (That recent years have not reversed this analysis could be demonstrated by the experience of many white teenagers in high school and by contrasting that experience with that of non-white, especially Asian, youth.)

If, as I argued from Walzer and Schaar, the structure of modern society makes it increasingly less necessary to participate in the collectivity since individuals are provided for in their individually considered problems, then the reality principle which found its justification in the production of necessary goods becomes in turn less necessary. If all or most of the same results (goods, etc.) can be obtained without the psychic costs, and since the collectivity was not very strong due to the particular nature of this reality principle, whatever solidary benefits were derived from the collectivity are not of sufficient strength that their loss would be noted.[64]

To what might the disintegration of the economic reality principle correspond conceptually? The economically focused reality principle requires that one be concerned about the future consequences of one's acts to the restriction of spontaneous gratification. This meant that one had to think about what one was likely to experience if one did a particular act at a particular time. The characteristic of such a mode of existence is that one finds it very difficult to live in the present, but instead must always be calculating about the future and worrying about the past. The time sense characteristic of such a form of existence is then highly linear: it must deny central importance to cyclical phenomena (such as weather, seasons), or find means to control them. The units by which it divides up the day must in principle be infinitely extendable without new characteristics arising. Clock sense is a prerequisite for the economic manner of thinking.

It has often been noted that the absence of a linear time sense is characteristic of preindustrial societies.[65] I am concerned here, however, with the consequences of the abandonment of a linear time sense in an already industrialized society—part of what we mean by a "post-industrial" society. In post-industrial society we would not expect to find the reemergence of a cyclical time sense, for such a society is not itself structured in a cyclical manner. (I am omitting here the possibility of simply leaving modern society, in the manner of some countercultural movements of fifteen to twenty-five years ago, a development the final success and possibility of which is not all clear.[66]) The time sense that an individual has must allow him or her to function in the society in which he or she is living.

What seems to happen among those who refuse or never have to learn the economic time frame is that, instead of developing a cyclical time sense, they develop an atomistic one in which moments are linked by neither social nor personal definition. (We see some of the consequences of this when children who have experienced no regularities come into school situations that demand artificial time rigidities.) Such a situation will often be referred to as "impulse" or "spontaneity" or "doing one's own thing" or possibly as "uncontrolled behavior"; in all cases it is a form of life which makes it very difficult to have extended and ongoing relations to others or to a collectivity. Hobbes knew as well as anyone that society is impossible unless one can know in some manner what the future is likely to be. (That he conceived of the possibilities as more narrow than they are in no way lessens the profundity of this insight.) In any case, the change in time sense characteristic of the movement from linear to atomistic time tends by itself to make permanent group relations much more difficult: about the only permanent relations one can have with such a sense are those of place. Yet place, as Nathaniel Hawthorne already knew in the nineteenth century, is too often sought for on a "celestial railroad": one is not happy where one is, unless one can put in the effort to be happy in a group. So one always seeks it somewhere else, and that search makes the finding impossible.

In addition to the change in time sense, there is also a change in the definition of what constitutes acceptable groups. Having a time sense which permitted having a past and a sense of the future (and of the shape of that future) also makes possible the acknowledgment of different kinds of authority. Political authority, as we have seen, is that form of relationship in which one accepts that another person knows in some situation better than oneself how one might proceed. The refusal to recognize that such relations can exist is the logical conclusion of those who cannot develop ongoing relations with others:

for it is true that in the moment all conclusions are equally valid. Truthfulness, or validity, is not possible except over time.

Hence, from such a perspective, all claims to authority must be perceived as essentially factional, that is, as attempts to assert a particular perspective. Now it is often fashionable to blame rebellious youth for a silly attitude towards authority.[68] Likewise contemporary rebellions are often praised because they question previously blindly accepted standards. Both of these attitudes seem ultimately mistaken in that they do not allow that both positions are only part of the story, taking themselves respectively to be all of it. In a social situation structured by an atomistic time sense, there can in fact be no authority, merely greater or lesser performance of those demands which individuals have been compelled to accept.

Herman Kahn and others[69] have described these and related developments as consequent to the lack of a goal in life. Yet this analysis, while surely descriptively correct, fails to penetrate the patina of facts. Goals are not something that people simply "give" themselves; they emerge rather from the welter of social circumstances which form the parameters for possible goals. One does not decide to be just anything, nor is the decision made in a vacuum. With this in mind one is tempted to say that the problems and developments I have been describing can be traced to the lack of a group, and this in turn to particular developments of the political and social world which originated in the politics of late nineteenth-century Europe.

The problem with Kahn's reaction (and others like it) is the implicit policy analysis involved. Most of these commentators see a solution to the problem of fading reality principle as merely the reverse of the trends which they analyze. But this, surely, must be another difficulty. It is hard to see why an act of will can resist what each of these analyses tells us (and with some accuracy) is the movement of a whole culture. Just as the society makes certain types of behavior more likely, so also, especially on the social scale, does it tend to render other types particularly difficult. Will is historical too.[70]

Take, for instance, the proposals of Herbert Marcuse. In a number of writings[71] he adopted a perspective which has its clear links to the argument advanced in this chapter. As he saw it, the dialectic has, for a variety of historically specific reasons, stopped; that is, the power to say "no" no longer functions in the same dynamic fashion in which it did in the past. The world has become "one dimensional." To this extent, we are unable as a society to benefit from the vastly expanded technology which will make it possible to substitute eros and leisure for the repression and toil of the present world.

There are two problems with this approach. First, Marcuse assumed that even though the definition of what is socially approved is given from social circumstances (and is thus not truly or completely human) that the same does not hold for the merely pleasurable. There is a tacit assumption that men do really know what makes them happy and that society does not define this, but can merely obfuscate it. Surely this is leftover Schillerian romanticism. I see no reason to assume that men and women will always *know* what makes them happy. Indeed the theoretical foundations on which one will premise such a claim seem dubious in the extreme. And simple observation of the particular qualities of restlessness — Hawthorne's celestial railroad — would indicate that many in the contemporary world are unable, at least to themselves and to others, to formulate precisely *what it is* that they might want. Hedonism is only a question when one knows what gives pleasure. The act of wanting does not necessarily entail the knowledge of what would constitute satisfaction. One may want nothing, and still thereby suffer from the nonrealization of potential.[72]

Second, the solution offered by a Marcuse (or a Kahn) imputes far too much independent energy to the human will. There is hidden here a streak of nineteenth-century volitionism, which holds that we need merely get properly down to it to be able to deal with our problems. One cannot simply oppose the movement of a culture without suffering at least the fate of Canute. (I should note that this does not mean that one *cannot* do anything, but one certainly cannot do *just* anything.)

The same problems appear in some of the work of Michael Walzer. At the end of "Radical Politics and the Welfare State" he calls for a "politics of insurgency" against the limitations imposed by the welfare state. He recognizes the need for an active public life; however, he does not provide us with any notion of the basis on which such insurgency might rest. His espousal of traditional social-democratic values is admirable. Since, however, he has shown that it is precisely the welfare state which is responsible for the demise of those values he would call back into being, why would an act of socialist and fraternal will resurrect those goals as the basis for a viable political force? It seems to me that Walzer has failed to take into account that historical developments of a particular kind might have made certain values and types of relationships among people simply no longer feasible.

I have asserted that a society whose groups are formed on the basis of the reality principle characteristic of Western industrialized societies will be able to maintain those groups only through a certain level of development. After that point has been reached, the ethic itself becomes nonrational, in the sense that the effort involved and the sacrifices observed no longer reasonably correspond to the rewards which are derived from those sacrifices. This disjuncture between individuals' perception of their action and the results leads to a breakdown of those group structures (collectivities) which permitted and were the focus of the political world. The central task of political theory or, more properly, of political theoretical writing is first to recognize that particular developments in the Western world are in the process of sharply reducing the availability of the arena of human action where human beings habitually dealt with each other in a political manner. This arena is not being replaced by something else. It is simply disappearing and this disappearance entails a diminution of the richness of available human experience. "The new development for our age cannot be political," wrote Kierkegaard with fine foresight in 1846, "for politics is a dialectical relationship between the individual and the community; but in our time the individual is in the process of becoming far too reflective to be able to be satisfied with being merely represented."[73]

There are two possibilities between which one can only stand. First, there is the possibility that political theory and politics might simply go the way of astrology, become another retrograde and somewhat fixed form of investigation which continues to be practiced, but is without significance in the world as we live it. This will be true not only for "political theory," but *a fortiori* for the subject matter of political theory, namely, politics, and of the attempt to bring order to the facts of politics, namely, political science. So much I hope to have already demonstrated in the previous chapter.

If this first possibility is in fact the case then there is really nothing to be done, for no one does govern. In such circumstances one would expect only an infinity of men and women feeling that they should live in communities with each other but in their very search for such community denying themselves the possibility of attaining community. The only alternative is withdrawal on the lines of that which Weber allows to those "who cannot bear the fate of the times like a man," a return to the open compassionate arms of encapsulated communities for "after all, they do not make it hard. . . ."[74]

A second possibility is that we are between periods of normal politics. If this is so, what we might be waiting for is a development which allows us to make some common sense — that is, sense which is ordinary and sense which is ours — out of our world. There are three ways in which theory has achieved an activist position,[75] although I do not think that any of these ways will be available in the future.

There could be a theory one might call transcendental (Hobbes, and in part Hegel), which would wipe away the muck of the ages and allow us to begin again. Such theory depends on an opposition to the historical. In the modern age, the historical has become transformed into atomistic organization where there is no real possibility of group; and, failing groups, there is no possibility of continuous time and thus no history.

Or there might be a theory, which one would call "historical," which seized a particular dynamic, a manner of using the past and not eliminating it. Such theory (Burke and in part Hegel) depends on the difference between volition and fact, on the possibility of grasping the powerful element of a time. If there is correspondence between will and fact (a stage which Hegel too sanguinely saw as the culmination of history), then there is no material for the historical theorist to deal with. And such correspondence was the aim of the rationalization of society—it, too, corresponded to the absence of group structure.

Finally, there might be a cyclical-reconstructive theory (like that of Arendt, Polybius, perhaps Marx) which would arise when there is historical change which produces a temporary vacuum, where not only the content of meaning but also the structures of meaning disappear. In the present day content does disappear, but not because the structures have changed, but rather that the structures have gradually emptied themselves out. The structures remain, though without the content, and men and women are left turning in a gyre which leads nowhere and provides no way out. Motion continues: people continue to search for community, but they do so in a manner which makes impossible the accomplishment of their design.

If all of this is true and we are at a stage between two kinds of normal politics, the coming world will be different from what we have experienced in the past. And so also will the ways in which we approach it. Previous manners of formulating the world into sense will no longer be effective — they merely repeat old tales. The next chapter attempts to make some sense out of what political theoretical writing would have to respond to.

5. Political Theory and the Parochial

For, dear me, why abandon a belief
Merely because it ceases to be true.
Cling to it long enough, and not a doubt
It will turn true again, for so it goes.
Most of the change we think we see in life
Is due to truths being in and out of favor.
                    Robert Frost,
                    "The Black Cottage"

In exploring the conditions of authority or community — of the "we" which stands as the basis of any community of discourse — I have considered three temptations that are particularly characteristic of the political realm, the temptations towards art, towards science, and towards a position of theoretical immaculateness.

I wish now in this last chapter to raise two interrelated matters. First, I want to argue for a parochial conception of authority; second, I want to suggest why this need not raise the specter of relativism; or, more accurately, I wish to examine why we think that the specter of relativism is raised.

We began with the question of the essential contestability of personhood. My perspective was contemporary, yet had its roots in Saint Augustine. In his *Confessions,* the first book to take the self so seriously that what it had to say about itself to God was important enough to merit being written down and published,[1] Augustine distinguishes among three faculties which together make up a person. The will is our faculty for shaping the future: it creates and forms that which we will be. Vision is our faculty for the present: it lets us see others and in turn be seen by them; it is the basis of the reciprocity

146

which is the foundation of politics. And memory is our faculty for shaping the past. All three of these faculties are determinative of self; the mystery of time incarnates them as a person. They lie under thought and reason, and they make them possible.

I have, in the course of this book, attempted to deconstruct the self along these lines. The characteristic mode of the theatrical was vision, the human faculty that gives us the presentness of others. The mode central to science was the faculty of will, our ability to make the future. And last, in the desire to be theoretically pure, there was a desire to control the past, an active and aggressive form of memory. These were Augustine's dimensions of the self.

There is always a tension among these three dimensions: in vision we are tempted to resolve that tension by theatricalizing our self; in will, the scientific temptation is to remove ourself from the world of which we are a part; and in the perversion of memory there is the temptation to theoretical assuredness, to be all powerful. To all of these temptations, the response was limitation, not to pose questions which we cannot answer, but not to ignore the temptations. Indeed, as Kant knew, there was no way to ignore them.[2]

It is then a mistake to think of the person as having at the center one thing, an essence. The person is a nexus of multiple times and spaces. I have been examining some of these dimensions over the course of this book and want now to pull together the themes of time and space around a possible vision of the political.

We might begin at the beginning. At the end of the *Republic*, in the myth of Er, we are presented with a vast array of souls choosing the self they will assume when they return to earth. Last to choose is Ulysses; there is but one soul left (Hades and the self are apparently zero-sum economies), but he declares himself pleased with his lot (as it now must be) and that he would have chosen it even if he had been first to choose. It is the lot of an ordinary man — I have always thought he would come back as Socrates. What is important is that in questions of the self, there is properly no choice; there is who we are and what is given to us, and the acceptance and willing of that is the end and the beginning of wisdom. At that point in the *Republic* the story ends, and the day begins. The task of political philosophy, we might say, has been to allow us to see for the first time who we are and to accept ourselves as our own.

We should look at what is given, not at what we have chosen from an apparently inexhaustible panoply of possibility, but at where or at what we are thrown. If one wanted to learn about oneself or someone else, one could do worse than to ask what places that person identifies him- or herself with. Places, and what happened in them, become the events that live in our lives; sometimes we call them symbols. In any case they serve to inform us of who we are. I remember the first hill I coasted down on my red wagon and my distress that it did not prove more dangerous.[3] That place or event still informs my anxieties about competence. Freud taught us to see the importance that casual, ordinary events have for our behavior — because we were someplace at some time (by accident, we were just there), we are different now.[4] This is not a reason to be terrorized by the ordinary the way the sociologist Erving Goffman is.

I turn first to an analysis of the ordinary space and time of life and its tensions and problems. I wish to do so in the context of American thought and literature — aided by some European friends — because I think our literature (the "we" again) is among the deepest in the world on these questions. Nowhere have the questions of the here and now, the ordinary, the everyday, been raised so complexly as in the United States. In this, Thoreau is the example to Heidegger and Nietzsche; Melville steals a march on Hegel, and Hawthorne makes Kant easier to read.[5]

Let us look at the question of the conception of the space we find ourself in. In American literature, place is constantly a problem, first defined by the fact that it is always being arrived at and left. Indeed, whether these places be numbing in their despair and ossification, or golden and embroidered with promise, it is the prevalent experience of having left them and arrived at them which has most centrally shaped the possibilities of our politics.

Even before capitalism rationalized motion and instrumentality as a form of life, Americans were a people of relentless travel. Whites gave up on where they were in search of something better, be it the next state or "the territories."[6] Blacks were first forced to move and later sought to escape the place and symbols of their past bondage; the same seems true now for browns. Importantly, we are dominated by an image of men and women both in escape from and in search of a place, of comings and goings.

The ambiguity and ambivalence that surrounds our pursuit of ordinary space is centrally symbolized by the particular role which our literature has reserved to the hometown. From Twain's Hannibal, Faulkner's Jefferson, and Lewis's Midwest, to the minutiae of sense of everyday Winesburg, Ohio, the hometown has been the central image of place in American thought and literature and life. In fact, despairing of what may be happening to them, we now build them in our Disneylands, even export them, perhaps to ensure their zoological preservation.

There is a strange ambivalence in the words themselves. Hometown: it is not just that it is the town in which our home is, but also that it is the town which is our home. "Hometown" is the answer sought by that archetypical American question: "where do you come *from?*" which we pose instead of "who are you?" or "what do you do?" In fact, the hometown is often assumed to be that place which we have left, or that in which we cannot stay. We think, for instance, ambivalently of the son who returns to live in his hometown, especially if he works at what his father did, certainly if the return is effectuated without the justification of prodigal time away. We even have a special category of marriage reserved for such individuals: the hometown sweetheart.[7]

I find myself in ambiguous relation to this concept. I grew

up in many places, most especially in Geneva, Switzerland (there are six Genevas in these United States), but I would never think of it as my hometown. So, as an American, which I am by ancestry and conviction, I do not come from anywhere and have had to make and then find my own. But the problems of place are paramount in American politics. Consider some of them.

Salem, Massachusetts, is the home of the Pyncheon family in Nathaniel Hawthorne's *The House of the Seven Gables*. The Pyncheons are a family like any other family, cursed by the greed for property, magnified in its fate only by its attempt to raise itself above others. Some of the family stay in the haunted ancestral house, accepting that it is their lot to perish. Others refuse this particular recognition of corruption and mortality and flee. Clifford Pyncheon, in particular, escapes, first to crime and punishment, and then again, at the end of the novel. This time he leaves by railroad, that great symbolic divider of American towns which for one hundred and fifty years now has kept those towns from being whole. The railroad always allows one to leave.

Clifford has boarded a train and purchased a ticket, Hawthorne tells us, for no direction in particular, just to ride for pleasure, as far as his money will take him. Called to accounts by a "gimlet eyed" old gentleman as to this strange mode of pleasure, Clifford claims that his pleasure is superior to the old staid ideas of fireside and home.

"In the name of common sense," asked the old gentleman, ". . . what can be better for a man than his own parlor and chimney corner?" Clifford replies that these things have not the merit which many good people attribute to them. . . . "My impression is that our wonderfully increased and still increasing facilities of locomotion are destined to bring us around again to the nomadic state."

Clifford goes on to argue that this time the nomadic state will have been perfected:

These railroads — could but the whistle be made musical and the rumble and jar gotten rid of — are positively the greatest blessing that the ages have wrought for us. They give us wings; they annihilate the toil and dust of pilgrimage; they spiritualize travel. Transition being so facile, what can man's inducement be to stay in one spot? Why therefore should he build a more cumbersome habitation than that which can readily be carried off with him? Why should he make himself a prisoner for life in brick and stone and worm-eaten timber, when in one sense he may easily dwell no-where — in a better sense, wherever the fit and beautiful shall offer him home?[8]

Well, why not? What is wrong with this vision of motor-homes and airplanes? Why, to take over Gertrude Stein's question, should there be a "there" there?

In this passage from Hawthorne, I read Clifford Pyncheon to be offering a conscious argument against a text which has served as a touchstone for this book. In the *Institutes of the Christian Religion,* Calvin writes:

> The earthly kingdom . . . I confess to be superfluous, if the kingdom of God, as it now exists within us, extinguishes the present life. But if it is the will of God that while we aspire to true piety, we are pilgrims on earth, and if such pilgrimage stands in need of such aids [as earthly government], then those who take them away from man rob him of his true humanity.[9]

The point of Calvin's argument is to show us, in the words of Samuel Beckett, that "we are on earth and there is no cure for *that.*"[10] The condition of what Calvin calls "pilgrimage" is one which asserts the validity of that which we have neither chosen nor had thrust upon us by others. It is an acceptance of a given spatiality of condition and a pursuit of that which will permit us to live in such a condition.

Clifford Pyncheon — the Clifford Pyncheon in us all — wants to "annihilate pilgrimage," to escape the possibility of being with others — the other — simply by an act of will. He discovers in the end that it is to no avail. As the railroad leads away, so the telegraph pursues him, reminding him of, without ever giving him, his past. What good will it do that he find himself in some strange town, only to discover that everyone is talking about the dead person whose blood is on his hands. America is fraught with those who sought someplace else to be someone, not in the grey plains of Kansas, but in the magical technicolor—the irreality—of somewhere over the rainbow.

The ability to live in one's own present instead repeatedly to seek a new future leads Americans to associate adulthood with adventure. At the end of Sherwood Anderson's *Winesburg, Ohio,* for instance, George Willard assumes that simply by leaving he will become a person.

> The young man's mind was carried away by his growing passion for dreams. One looking at him would not have thought him particularly sharp. With the recollection of little things occupying his mind he closed his eyes and leaned back on the railroad car seat. He stayed that way for a long time and when he aroused himself and again looked out of the car window the town of Winesburg had disappeared and his life there had become but a backdrop on which to paint the dreams of manhood.[11]

This, the promise of will and adventure, the promise of making something out of oneself, is tied to a fatal notion of the individual that we have inherited from the Enlightenment. The promise is bound to fail. It is but a few decades from George Willard's expectations to these reflections by the French philosopher Jean-Luc Nancy:

> The individual is only the residue of the proof of the dissolution of community. By his nature—as the name indicates, he is an atom, an indivisible—the individual reveals that he is the abstract result of a decomposition. He is the symmetrical match of the immanent: the absolutely detached for-itself, taken as origin and as certainty.[12]

The vision of the individual by himself, self- and sense-certain, is the promise of adventure and of will. It is, in American literature at least, repeatedly unsatisfied and unrewarded.

And in that literature we see also that one of the usual solutions is equally flawed. Here again the hometown — where you come from — is the problem. Midway through Herman Melville's *Israel Potter* (an obscure novel, about a "plebian Lear," as Melville calls him), the hero finds himself in service under John Paul Jones on the *Bonhomme Richard*. In an engagement with a British frigate, he is caught up on the bowsprit of the British ship and suddenly finds himself aboard it. No one, of course, knows who he is, and he thinks it best to keep his peace about being an American. The British ship, however, in stark contrast to the American, has no place for someone without a place. In a grotesque slapstick, Melville portrays Potter as led from work gang to work gang in order to determine where he belongs. At last the captain intervenes:

> Some fifteen minutes passed, when the captain coming from his cabin and observing the master-at-arms leading Israel about in this indefinite style demanded the reason of that procedure, adding that it was against his express orders that any new and degrading punishment be invented for his men. "Come here, master-at-arms. To what end do you lead that man about?" "To no end in the world, sir. I am leading him because he has no final destination."[13]

Israel spends fifty years in exile, looking for America and his place: he is friend and servant to the important, plays a decisive though completely unknown role in the Revolutionary War, and, still without a place, returns at the end of his life to his birthplace to find that neither he, nor his family, is remembered and that the ground has been plowed over.

Why has this theme of the return home so controlled much of our literature? It is the recognition that not all solutions to the problem of the spatial definition of self are equivalent solutions, the point I made about Locke. For Hawthorne and the others, the hometown is a bad solution to the question of the other. In the hometown one *is* seen: that is both its seduction and its terror. But one is seen too easily: the recognition is too indulgent. One's vices are as much as anything else a claim to community (the town drunk). "Home," Robert Frost wrote, "is the place where, when you go there, they have to take you in." Comforting though that is in that one is reminded that there are things one does not deserve, "having" to be taken in can be dangerous. The self of *this* community is bound by all that is transitory and common in our lives. The love-ties to our families, which we chose not; the seductive street corners that framed our first disobediences; the parking lots and lanes which masked our first incompetent erotic fumblings: to make these the flesh of our bodily lives is to live only with our aging and our past, never our present, never ourselves. The hometown — the community for which it stands — is an indulgence of our childhood and our adolescence. We have not grown up if it is in this place that we meet others. We need it, however, as something to move away from, to know that we have broken the ties of blood that kept us children and that we have the courage to confront our sins, our virtues, and ourselves.

Let us look now at the other dimension of the self, that of time. The temporal analogue to the hometown has been the city which lies down the road, at the end of the yellow brick pavement to adventure.

Dorothy goes on such an adventure, and she is even accompanied by a populist alliance of workers and farmers and politicians. She finds that in the city that lies at the end of the road one meets not the answer, but merely the same old neighbors on the same quest. "'You're a very bad man,' cried Dorothy. 'Oh, no,' replied the terrible Oz, 'I'm not a bad man at all; I'm just a very bad wizard.'" Cities require wizards. No one has to take you in, in a city: that is why they are the space of adventure. But they are, in our country, I am afraid, increasingly the place where one can hide from the other, where one's own weakness and vices never need be apparent to others. One is there alone, in the end. And one may do what one wants because what one does is of no necessary importance to anyone else. If to be a person is to be seen by another — as philosophers from Hobbes to Rousseau and Hegel to Wittgenstein tell us — then the modern city — I do not call it a polis — makes it unnecessary to be a person.

I have suggested faulty ways of construing the past and present in one's life. Yet there is also a memory which is a continual refounding of the present, its "noble form." In a passage we have seen before, Maurice Merleau-Ponty refers to

the fine word *Stiftung* — foundation, establishment — [which] designates those operations of culture which open a tradition, continue to have value after their historical appearance, and require beyond themselves acts both other and the same, in which they perpetually come to life again and again. . . . [This tradition is], as Husserl remarks, the power to forget origins, to begin again differently to give to the past not a survival, which is a hypocritical form of forgetfulness, but the efficacy of repetition or life, which is the noble form of memory.[14]

Such memory lies deeper than the assessments which it makes possible. "Memory believes," wrote Faulkner, "before knowing remembers." He wrote that in *Light in August,* a book that has its time in the absolute moment in which the pure space of the present is born. We *are,* he shows us, before we make anything of it.

Perhaps the automatic quality of such "noble" memory will jar and annoy. But it is designed to remind us that no one becomes a person by trying to be one. *"We" and "I" cannot be the result of a project.* Look again at Hawthorne. In *The Blithedale Romance,* a novel about place, friendship, and the destruction wrought by the intentional pursuit of self and community, he wrote that those who

incorporate themselves into an over-ruling purpose, finally are converted to little else save that one principle. Such men had no heart, no sympathy, no reason, no conscience. They keep no friend, unless he make himself the mirror of their purpose . . . and [they] will smite and slay you the more readily if you take the first step with them and cannot take the second. . . .[15]

The person is thus a by-product of activity, not its goal. To the degree that one sets out to make something of oneself, one is, as Max Weber wrote, no person at all. Personhood has to be the result of an accident — or rather a series of them. Central to a person are the accidents of place, the taking upon oneself of the mystery of things.

I place importance here on the notion of accident because we live in a world that has increasingly sought to make accident less possible. The logic of technology, of power based on knowledge, is to resist failure and unpredictability. It is a safe world which would eradicate the nerve to fail, because it is too often a world in which the nerve has failed. A person, however, is made up of the sense given to the myriad moments and minutiae of experience that make up time. "You are what you pretend to be," wrote Kurt Vonnegut, "therefore be careful about what you pretend."[16]

How then is sense given to our past? In the Platonic dialogue which bears his name, Protagoras argues to Socrates that men have politics due to an oversight. After creation, Zeus had given to Epimetheus the task of handing out to each creature those qualities which would have made it both specific and capable of survival — its particular *arete*. Due to Epimetheus' dullness, when he got at last to human beings, everything had been given away and nothing was left whereby humans might protect and fend for themselves. Even the theft of fire in an act of generous desperation by Epimetheus' brother Prometheus was not sufficient, and Zeus had to send Hermes back on a special mission to give each human the ability to live with others. According to Protagoras, then, it is the lack of the natural qualities of survival which require that men live together. Politics for Protagoras rests on necessity. The question which immediately comes to mind and which forms the center of the dialogue is how men shall in coming generations acquire the knowledge and virtue of how to live with each other. Protagoras argues that the best master is prudence and learning from experience. It is on lessons based from the past that he seeks to demonstrate that virtue can be taught and the state made to prosper.

During the course of their exchange, reeling under the obvious truth of Protagoras' position, Socrates appears to adopt several positions. Finally, he allows that the problem has not been solved and indicates as he breaks off that he prefers Prometheus to Protagoras' Epimetheus. Prometheus — the name means forethought — provides a model for the transformation of the human condition. We know his fate. Epimetheus — the name means afterthought — provides a model for prudence and preservation of the past. We know that Epimetheus is the person who persuaded Pandora to open the box of evils on the world. Socrates seems to be indicating that if our memory of the past is *only* prudential — that is, composed of that which we have, from experience, learned not to do, we will in ourselves repeat only the lessons of past pains and pleasures. If, instead, we come to know and speak of ourselves in tension with the vision of a future condition, then we will not learn from the past what to do in our future — there is nothing to be so learned that is alive — rather we will learn that it is from a vision of the future that our past can be recovered. That which has *happened* to *each* of us divides us from the other; that which is a vision of what can be puts us into a community of discourse that leads us to acknowledge others. An activity undertaken, a common activity, creates a past for us which we would not have otherwise had. It is the source of the answer to the fundamental political question, "who are *we*?" Part of the nostalgia which is sometimes evidenced both in word and deed by my generation for the "sixties" comes from the mistaken sense that only then, all could be made new. This sense is mistaken because all *can* at all moments be made new: that is what we mean by a sacrament. "Let your whole life be a baptism," wrote Luther in his *Tabletalk.*

The perversion of vision derives from the temptation to transform it into power. Hawthorne again spoke to this point. In a short Faust story called "The Birthmark," he gives us a man of science, proficient in all branches of natural philosophy, and recently married. He has trouble disengaging his love for knowledge and his love for an other, for his wife. He thus desires to remove the one blemish that keeps his wife from natural perfection, a small birthmark on her cheek in the shape of a hand. For Hawthorne, it is that hand by which mortality keeps her human. The husband desires to make her perfect by his science, and finally succeeds. He finds that perfection is not for this earth and his wife dies from her perfection. Imperfection, Hawthorne tells us, is the condition of living with others.

Faust has been with us longer than the bourgeoisie, even if he only began to reinvest in the early nineteenth century. In *Ecclesiastes,* that strange book about this earth, we find: "I saw vanity under the sun: a person who has no one, either brother or sister, yet there is no end to his toil and his eyes are never satisfied with riches, so that he never asks 'For whom am I toiling and depriving myself?' This also is vanity and an unhappy business." The preacher goes on to assert that "Two are better than one because they have a good reward for their toil."

They have as reward, in other words, each other, and not the world that they have made and shaped with their knowledge and power and toil. The only life that is a free life is the life with another, for only another can be freely (and must be freely) chosen. Such a being with an other requires that one has freed oneself, for a time at least, from that which holds us to the necessities—as opposed to the accidents—of this world, from the awe-ful ties of eros, from the monster of history. It is certainly a phenomenon of the modern world that such a vision is less and less attainable. In our age, to claim honestly to have freed oneself from this world is more and more difficult.

The reasons for this were best laid out by Max Weber. In *Economy and Society* he wrote:

> Bureaucracy develops the more perfectly, the more it is 'dehumanized,' the more completely it succeeds in eliminating from official business love, hatred, and all purely personal, irrational and emotional elements which escape calculation.[17]

Weber understood the development of bureaucracy to be the front of a great historical process of rationalization that has as its consequence the increasing destruction of affective or status relations between persons and the progressive domination of the economic over the political.[18] The bureaucrat is the vanguard of the historical process, implicitly a participant in a vast revolutionary process which will totally transform all human relationships. To live by the division of labor as a member of a rationalized bureaucratic structure, is, Weber says explicitly, not to be a person, but it is to participate in the most widespread revolutionary process in the world. Marx had argued in *The Communist Manifesto* that it was the nature and glory of the bourgeoisie to wipe out all structures that threaten to become permanent. "All that is solid melts into thin air," he wrote, signifying that the Faustian urge now central to the bourgeoisie would tolerate nothing to remain in the form that it was in, neither human relations nor commodities.[19] Weber's vision is a cousin to that of Marx, except that for him the solids that melt (love, passion, hatred, marriage, honor, etc.) are specifically the manners in which one is present to another and not just the predicates to the stages prior to the bourgeoisie.

Weber thus implies that under no foreseeable conditions will humans be able to live in other than rationalized, "demagified," society. This is the "steel box" (or iron cage) of the end of the book on the Protestant ethic.

This is the world which Nietzsche characterized as living after the "death of God." He meant that humans are unable to make serious contact with a world that transcends their own activity, and that being unable to free ourselves from this world, each step we undertake to so attempt merely confirms our own prison. This is also why Nietzsche and others thought that the death of God might make a political life once again possible.

What then would be the dynamics of the recognition and acknowledgment of the other, of the conditions of authority and community that are the stuff of politics and the task of political theory? It is here that we see the importance of shared vision which I discussed above. To share vision with another involves the capacity to have a particular sentiment, now much out of favor. I would call it by its old name, guilt. It means not that we are ashamed at how we appear before each other, but that we are able to recognize our failures to live up to a vision that we share. The other is a reminder of that failure, of a failure for which there is no excuse.

In this sense, the possibility of guilt takes us beyond the realm of morality, into the realm of politics. Morality, as Kant taught us, requires that the normative act be possible. Politics — the acknowledgment and recognition of a "we" as a solution to the problems of the "I" — *requires precisely that the norms which bind us together not be possible.* You cannot plead excuses in politics; "I am sorry" is not a political utterance. When Hannah Arendt wrote at the end of her book on Adolf Eichmann that "politics is not the nursery," she meant that no excuses could be offered. It is the fact that we cannot offer excuses that makes the act political rather than ethical. It is the fact that the vision of what should be is unattainable and that I accept it as our vision and in doing so find myself wanting that generates the free community.

I am thus claiming for politics and the vision of the political person something that will not always sit easily: that to be a member of a free community, one has to accept as true for oneself the proposition that at certain times in fact and always in principle, someone may know better than one does oneself just how it is with oneself. This is, of course, what Rousseau was trying to express by the general will and the consequent notion of being forced to be free.

But who may know? Surely, you will respond, not just anyone. Indeed not. But also not someone to whom one has gone looking for an answer. (Oracles are pre- and perhaps postpolitical.) As examples, let me offer two cases. The first are the words which John Winthrop spoke, like Moses to the Hebrews outside the promised land, to those assembled on board the *Arabella,* ready to take possession of the American Israel.

The only way to avoid shipwreck and to provide for posterity, Winthrop says

> is to follow the counsel of Micah: to do justly, to love mercy, to walk humbly with our God. For this end, we *must* be knit together in this work as one man; we *must* entertain each other in brotherly affection; . . . we must delight in each other, make others' conditions our own, rejoice together, mourn together, labor and suffer together, having always before our eyes our commission and community in the work, our community as members of the same body.[20]

These are not the lines from this famous sermon that Ronald Reagan was fond of quoting. Winthrop continues that as long as we keep our eyes on our work, as long as our vision is true and in front of us, we will surely be blessed. But if we turn aside "we will surely perish out of the good land whither we pass over this vast sea to possess it."

The elements of memory, vision, and willful activity are the articulations of Winthrop's claim about political community and the persons who live in it. It was a choice made by each to serve God (*this* God) and a sense that this choice was more bracing by its justice than any other. Puritan chroniclers delighted in citing the book of Joshua to their more timid Anglican brethren: "Choose ye this day which God you will serve." It is a choice — all is known — not a subject for research. And the implication is that were we not to choose we would fail in God's task and become a servant not to ourselves and justice, but to "our pleasures and our profits," as Winthrop put it.

Another example, closer in time and space. During the 1950s and 1960s, groups of blacks and whites sat in at lunch counters in the South with the aim of changing the laws that forbade such integration. It would be usual, but wrong, to say that they were trying to "impose" or "convince" the racist white owners of their point of view. It would also be wrong — though, of course, not inaccurate — to claim that they were trying to make nonintegration so costly that the owners would see economic rationality.[21] Rather those who sat in were trying to demonstrate to the owners that they—the owners—insofar as they were in fact American, actually accepted or were bound to acknowledge that lunch counters should be integrated. The demonstrators were trying to show the owners something about themselves, and to do so in such a manner that the claim had to be acknowledged or else the person to whom the claim was addressed would have to change who he or she was.

At this level, politics is a risky business, a kind of Pascalian wager on personhood. Were the demonstrators wrong, they would have been so informed by history, or the courts, or death. Some never found out.

And with this, we have returned to the question of the first chapter, the status of the "we" which serves as authority and makes politics possible. I suggested that the "we" which serves as authority in politics and to the discovering of when political theory is addressed stands in tension with the various time and space dimensions of which it can be an intersection. It is drawn towards other communities of discourse; it must treat them as temptations, important for the acknowledgment of an essentially contested person, but not to be yielded to. I finally have just suggested that this "we" was notably different from the "we" of morality in that the vision which held the moral "we" together was necessarily possible, while this one was necessarily impossible.

More is at stake than it might seem. If a vision is possible—attainable in principle—then it is attainable for everyone. The basic egalitarianism which we saw implicit in the "we" entails that. But if the "we" is parochial, limited to the particular people with whom one finds oneself at this particular time and in this particular place—this is what it means to have a body—then the question is raised of the status of that "we." What is to stop anything from being a "we"? This is the problem of relativism.

A contemporary theorist who has addressed himself to this problem on a repeated basis, Michael Walzer, in his recent *Exodus and Revolution*,[22] has suggested that a just commonwealth is founded on deliverance from bondage even more than it

might be founded on some principle of justice. We can, he
suggests, collectively and willfully pursue simply a better place
than we are in now; that we fail to attain perfection is not a
cause for despair. The argument is elegant and honest. Yet,
why was it that the Hebrews and only the Hebrews sought
deliverance from Egypt and sought it for themselves only?
Walzer's answer contains two elements. A first step was the
experience of oppression; a second was the covenant. In this
answer, at least in Walzer's presentation of it, becoming a people is something willed or agreed to and memorialized. "So
pharaonic oppression, deliverance, Sinai and Canaan are still
with us, powerful memories shaping our perception of the political world."[23]

One might be tempted to retort that this is casuistry, case
by case analysis. And so it is; nor does that seem bad to me.
But the specter is raised of how do we know that this "we" is
acceptable? What is to stop—in the end the argument always
comes back to this—Nazi Germany from claiming they are
a "we." [Note that Walzer can respond that this is not the problem for him.]

Someone might make the following accusation:

> Look at your definition of authority. It consists in being
> able to find another in me, and myself in another. It con-
> sists in what you, following Emerson called "provocation."
> Now, that is all very well, but you have not given any cri-
> teria that transcend the immediate, the here and now. On
> what grounds do you claim this for yourself? What is to
> stop someone else from claiming awful things. Suppose I
> found Hitler in myself?[24]

The claim against relativism—let us mean ethical relativism—rests on the claim that it is possible to give for any moral
judgment a universal generalization of that judgment. That
is, the claim that "Charlie ought to keep his promise to meet
Cynthia at three o'clock on Tuesday" must entail and be entailed by the sentence that "One ought to keep promises."[25]
Yet if we take the second general sentence to be a sentence

that someone might utter, it is hard to find a situation in ordinary life in which it actually performs the work that ethical theorists wish it to perform. If you actually ask the question "why ought I to keep my promises?" you are in effect asking a question which raises doubts about the necessity of honoring claims that others are making on you. In life, therefore, the move to universalization is a move which reflects a *doubt* about the other, i.e., which raises a question about the authority of a "we." Hence politics gives us the parochial.

This short analysis gives a sense of what morality is supposed to do. It is a way of resolving the anxieties about the other, by avoiding the tenuousness of the specific relationship and replacing it by a relationship to persons in general. Whether or not this move is possible, it is clear that human relationships are changed by making this move. Whether or not there are universals in human life,[26] there is a difference in being in relation with a universal as opposed to, what I shall call here, a particular.

The political — the acknowledgment of a specific historical given other — is thus necessarily parochial, and ultimately, though not necessarily, in conflict with the demands of morality. Let me look briefly here at some of the costs of holding to the absolute demands of morality, what Stanley Cavell has called the "moralization of morality." I want to suggest that at times when the normal notion of a person is essentially contested, morality itself must also be understood as possibly open to repudiation. I am nervous about this, for fear of misunderstanding and being misunderstood.

I want to say that when I do not find myself in you — when the conditions of political authority are not present — the possibility or the desirability of a moral rendering of our relationship disappears. To *attempt* to so render our relationship will be destructive. This does not call morality into question so much as it indicates that we must first resolve the political theoretical question — that of authority and the other — before we can render our world in moral terms.

It is no accident, therefore, that modern literature is filled

with scenes in which the repudiation of morality is the necessary step to the establishment of a self. (This is clearly what
was on Nietzsche's mind when he spoke of a position "beyond
good and evil" and Kierkegaard of the "teleological suspen-
sion of the ethical.") What bothered Nietzsche was that the
resort to ethical argument — to claims of good and evil — when
the conditions of authority and the self were radically contested could be at the source of great disasters. Cavell writes:

> Someday, if there is a someday, we will have to learn that
> evil thinks of itself as good, that it could not have made
> much progress in the world unless people planned and per-
> formed it in all conscience.[27]

Political theory makes it possible to say "who is to say" when
and how it is possible to be moral — or better, allows us to recognize it. It was to political theory in action that Weber looked
when he queried in "Politics as a Vocation": "Who is entitled
to place his hands on the wheel of history?"[28] That Weber
thought that what previously had been accomplished by beliefs
must now be accomplished by an incarnate text — a political
hero — tells us something of the strengths and weaknesses of
his analysis of modernity.

My claims about the limited sphere of morality — or Weber's
claims about the plebiscitarian Caesar — should not be taken
to imply that any one, for any reason, at any time, can claim
to be outside the sphere of morality. Even Nietzsche, who was
if anything too obsessed about the iron cage of morality, closes
his long analysis of the genealogy of morality with the statement that it is when humans think they are escaping morality
that they will be at their most moral. All of the great thinkers
of the early part of this century, most of whom share the kinds
of concerns I have sketched out here, spend a great deal of
time elaborating the conditions under which a political actor
can claim entitlement to exemption from the demands of morality — and this is as true for V. I. Lenin as it is for Weber
or, indeed, for Freud.

Let me, in the end, come back to a case not unlike that

of the "womb for rent" which I raised in the first chapter. It is clear that technology has radically changed the way we think about abortion, and will continue to do so. Technology has made it impossible to claim that abortion should be forbidden on the grounds that it endangers the health of the mother. Soon we will see a situation in which the easy, court-ordained division of the prenatal existence of a fetus into trimesters of survivability no longer makes very much sense.

So one wants to ask: As what is the fetus being treated in an abortion? Those who oppose abortion want a moral resolution to the question of abortion — a universal, non-case specific, non-parochial answer. They want to treat the fetus as a person, on the grounds that it is human.[29] Human — rather than, shall I say, canine — the fetus certainly is. Yet do we not also treat humans as something other than persons, at times at least? Take for example the citation from Weber used before:

> Bureaucracy develops the more perfectly, the more it is 'dehumanized,' the more completely it succeeds in eliminating from official business love, hatred, and all purely personal, irrational and emotional elements which escape calculation.[30]

I should note that most of us are quite happy with this non-politicization of human relationships: picture yourself in line to pay a bill and being told by the cashier that he didn't like you and wouldn't take your money. In the abortion case, however, we are ill at ease. As what is the embryo treated? One answer would be that it is treated *as an embryo*. Well, what does that entitle you to? The *moral* answer to that question is, I submit, not obvious, and it is not obvious because we do not have an adequately resolved question of person for these cases, i.e., we have not solved the *political* question.

And so, we must resolve the specific case, which is, I think, the only way that we can resolve abortion questions — indeed, all those questions that present themselves to us in a political manner. We must deal with the parochial, the here and now, the limited. These are not universal questions, but they must be our questions. Who is carrying the embryo? What is the social, educational, economic status of the person? What does she know? Why does she want the abortion? What shame in this society would attach itself to this birth? What consequences are there for others in the parent's (singular and plural) life? That these political questions, for people in this society, are often answered in support of abortion, does not mean that we have an argument in favor of abortion. In fact, quite the contrary, we should not seek an argument in favor of abortion—a moral resolution, a last word—to the question, even and especially if we accept the necessity of abortions in this society, for our people, at this time in our history. In this we abjure perfection, we make possible our humanity again. We are not such stuff as dreams are made of.

Here is the role and the greatness of politics and of political theory which makes that politics available to us. It gives us a first word. We have only to resist wanting the last.

NOTES

1. POLITICAL THEORY AND CRISIS

1. The notion of a mode of discourse is Michael Oakeshott's in *Rationalism in Politics* (New York: Basic Books, 1962), pp. 197–247, and in *On Human Conduct* (Oxford: Clarendon, 1975) especially Part I. Related concepts are found in the notion of story or narrative in Alasdair MacIntyre, *After Virtue* (London: Duckworth, 1982), and in his *Against the Self-Images of the Age* (London: Duckworth, 1971), pp. 260–279; in the idea of an "essentially contested concept" which William Connolly in *The Terms of Political Discourse* (Lexington, Mass.: Heath, 1974) borrows from W. G. Gallie, and in the general notion of a language as elaborated by Charles Taylor, *Philosophical Papers* (Cambridge: Cambridge University Press, 1986), vol. I, pp. 213 ff, and vol. II, pp. 15–57.

2. On life as autobiography see Alexander Nehamas, *Nietzsche, Life as Literature* (Cambridge, Mass.: Harvard University Press, 1982). For my disagreements with this reading of Nietzsche see my "Nietzsche's Political Aesthetics," in *Towards New Seas: Nietzsche on Philosophy, Aesthetics and Politics,* ed. Michael A. Gillespie and Tracy B. Strong (Chicago: University of Chicago Press, 1988).

3. On meta-narratives see W. J. T. Mitchell, *On Narrative* (Chicago: University of Chicago Press, 1986). See Michel Foucault, "Nietzsche, Genealogy and History" in *Language, Counter-Memory and Practice* (Ithaca, N.Y.: Cornell, 1980), pp. 139–164. See my analysis in "Texts and Pretexts: Reflections on Perspectivism in Nietzsche," in my *Friedrich Nietzsche and the Politics of Transfiguration,* Expanded Edition (Berkeley and Los Angeles: University of California Press, 1988). See also Derek Parfit, *Reasons and Persons* (Oxford: Oxford University Press, 1986). On a link between Parfit and Nietzsche, see Bart Schultz, "Persons, Selves and Utilitarianism," *Ethics* 96, 4 (July 1986): 721–745, especially 744–745. Parfit himself uses a quote from Nietzsche as epigraph.

4. Interestingly, the question was almost never posed the other way around. There is, however, a tradition coming out of Kantian

moral theory and ordinary language philosophy which would imply that because I ought to do something, it follows that the world is structured in such a way as to make it possible for me to do it.

5. See Talcott Parsons, *The Structure of Social Action* (New York: McGraw-Hill, 1937).

6. See the discussion by Judith N. Shklar, "Snobbery," *Ordinary Vices* (Cambridge, Mass.: Harvard University Press, 1986).

7. Probably the key texts here are Stephen Toulmin, *Reason in Ethics* (Cambridge: Cambridge University Press, 1968) and Kurt Baier, *The Moral Point of View* (Ithaca, N.Y.: Cornell University Press, 1958) and the title essay in Stanley Cavell, *Must We Mean What We Say?* (New York: Scribners' Sons, 1969). Somewhat later a whole set of books sought to examine the importance of Wittgenstein for political and social thought. First, and to my mind still the best among these, was Hanna F. Pitkin, *Wittgenstein and Justice* (Berkeley and Los Angeles: University of California Press, 1972). See also James Tully, "Wittgenstein and Political Philosophy," *Political Theory* (May 1989).

8. See, classically, John Rawls, "Two Kinds of Rules," *Philosophical Review* 64 (1955); Stanley Cavell on "categorical declaratives" in *Must We Mean What We Say?*, chap. 1, p. 31. See the critique of this move in Cavell, *The Claim of Reason: Wittgenstein, Skepticism, Morality, and Tragedy* (Oxford: Clarendon, 1979), chap. 11.

9. The example is drawn from conversations with Terence Ball.

10. In fact, Cavell was, as his later writings made clear, not quite engaged in this boundary-drawing; but his original work was often taken to indicate that he was.

11. See Peter Winch, *The Idea of a Social Science* (London: Routledge and Kegan Paul, 1958); Winch's claims have been criticized and examined in *Rationality,* ed. Bryan Wilson (Evanston, Ill.: Harper and Row, 1971), especially the essay by Alasdair MacIntyre. See also MacIntyre, *After Virtue,* pp. 244–258. See also Alan Ryan, *Philosophy of Social Sciences* (New York: Pantheon, 1970) and Pitkin, *Wittgenstein and Justice,* pp. 241–264.

12. See R. G. Collingwood, *An Essay on Metaphysics* (Chicago: University of Chicago Press, 1972); *An Autobiography* (Oxford: Oxford University Press, 1964). See also Stephen Toulmin, "Conceptual Revolutions in Science," in *Boston Studies in the Philosophy of Science,* vol. 3, ed. R. Cohen and M. Wartofsky (Dordrecht: Reidel, 1966), pp. 331–347.

13. On the notion of a metaphor taking, see Clifford Geertz, "Ideology as a Cultural System," in *The Interpretation of Cultures* (New York: Basic Books, 1973).

14. See the discussion in Strong, *Friedrich Nietzsche and the Politics of Transfiguration,* Epilogue.

15. The first text to present a convincing argument that fascism was the possible culmination of developments in Western civilization was Karl Polanyi, *The Great Transformation* (Chicago: University of Chicago Press, 1944).

16. The reference is to the title of the well-known and important textbook by Samuel Beer and Adam Ulam, *Patterns of Government.*

17. For some of the sources of confusion in Kuhn's usage, see the critique of his uses of the word "paradigm" in Margaret Masterman's contribution to *Criticism and the Growth of Knowledge,* ed. I. Lakatos and R. Musgrave (Cambridge: Cambridge University Press, 1970).

18. See Stanley Milgram, *Obedience to Authority* (New York: Harper and Row, 1974), especially pp. 179–189. Other important works in this genre include Bruno Bettelheim, "Individual and Mass Behavior in Extreme Situations," *Journal of Abnormal and Social Psychology* 38, 4 (Oct. 1943): 417–452 and his book, *The Informed Heart* (Glencoe, Ill.: Free Press, 1960) as well as the Kafkaesque world of Erving Goffman in *Asylums* (Garden City, N.Y.: Anchor Books, 1961).

19. The ring of Gyges offered invisibility to its bearer and thus has served as a paradigm test as to whether or not one would engage in base actions when there is no chance of being caught. See Rousseau's discussion in the *Discourse on the Origins of Inequality.* In fact, most of those who found themselves attracted to Marx, Nietzsche, and Freud failed to see the degree to which each of these theorists also subjected his own text to the critique which he launched on others. Properly, therefore, these theorists offer the temptation of Gyges, but also teach us to refuse it. See chapter two for a discussion of this.

20. See the discussion in Stanley Cavell, *Themes Out of School* (Chicago: University of Chicago Press, 1984), pp. 45–48.

21. See Charles Taylor, "Neutrality in Political Science," in *Philosophical Papers,* vol. 2, pp. 58–90.

22. As tries, for instance, Thierry Maulnier in *Violence et conscience* (Paris: Gallimard, 1945).

23. Thus Lenin sees it necessary to criticize *every* aspect of his opponents, and the once true comrade Kautsky has to be declared a "renegade." See my discussion in "Entitlement and Legitimacy: Weber and Lenin on the Problems of Leadership" in *Constitutional Democracy: A Festschrift for Henry Ehrmann,* ed. Fred Eidlin (Boulder, Colo.: Westview Press, 1983), pp. 174–175. For an interpretation of Stalinism in these terms, see the brilliant essay by Sheila Fitzpatrick, "Cultural Revolution as Class War," in *Cultural Revolution in Russia, 1928-1931* (Bloomington, Ind.: Indiana University Press,

1984). For a good account of more recent times see James Miller, *Democracy is in the Streets* (Chicago: Basic, 1986).

24. Some, such as Michael Walzer and Bernard Williams, have consciously abandoned the search for general principles as misdirected. See chapter five.

25. See Allan Megill, *Prophets of Extremity* (Berkeley: University of California Press, 1985) and his essay in *What Should Political Theory Be Now?* ed. John Nelson (New York: New York University Press, 1983) and my parallel essay "Nihilism and Political Theory" in that volume. See also the very interesting book by Gillian Rose, *The Dialectic of Nihilism* (Oxford: Basil Blackwell, 1984), who, like Megill, has some of the same villains, but also some different heroes.

26. See Sheldon S. Wolin, "Political Theory as a Vocation," in *Machiavelli and the Nature of Political Thought,* ed. Martin Fleischer (New York: Atheneum, 1972), pp. 23–75.

27. See Michael Walzer, "On the Role of Symbolism in Political Thought," *Political Science Quarterly* 81, 3 (June 1967): 191–204, especially pp. 198–199.

28. Friedrich Nietzsche, *Ecce Homo,* "Why I Write such good Books," 1.

29. The term was, I believe, Robert Dahl's in 1957 and betrays the influence of developments such as those I have just sketched.

30. The early positivists sought to develop a perfectly human world, under human control, after a successful battle against the dark forces of the irrational and obfuscatory. That such knowledge was a sin against nature was not a strong trait in their American followers.

31. P. Laslett and W. D. Runciman, *Philosophy, Politics and Society,* 1st and 2nd series (Oxford: Basil Blackwell, 1956).

32. Leo Strauss, *Natural Right and History* (Chicago: University of Chicago Press, 1953); *Persecution and the Art of Writing* (Glencoe, Ill.: Free Press, 1952); see Allan Bloom, *The Closing of the American Mind* (New York: Basic, 1986).

33. Eric Voegelin, *The New Science of Politics* (Chicago: University of Chicago Press, 1966).

34. See John Gunnell, *Political Theory: Tradition and Interpretation* (Cambridge, Mass.: Winthrop, 1979) and the exchange with John Pocock in the *Annals of the American Academy of Political and Social Science* (1980).

35. Connolly, *The Terms of Political Discourse.*

36. Ibid, p. 35. Younger readers may perhaps not recognize the reference to the scene in the movie *Five Easy Pieces,* in which Jack Nicholson's inability to order a chicken salad sandwich without all that came with it leads to complete mayhem.

37. Ibid., pp. 38–39.

38. Compare on this point Cavell, *Must We Mean What We Say?* p. 21: "What is normative is exactly ordinary use itself."

39. R. W. Emerson, *Essays and Lectures* (New York: Library of America, 1983), p. 79.

40. William Shakespeare, *King Lear,* Act IV, Scene 2. See Cavell, *Must We Mean What We Say?* chap. nine; and L. Wittgenstein, *On Certainty* (Oxford: Basil Blackwell, 1969), #378: "Knowledge is in the end based on acknowledgement."

41. See my "Nietzsche's Political Aesthetics" in *Towards New Seas.*

42. David Hume, "Of the Original Contract," in *Theory of Politics,* ed. F. Watkins (Edinburgh, N.Y.: Nelson, 1951), p. 145. See the parallel comments in Cavell, *Claim of Reason,* pp. 22–23. The language in the next paragraph is shaped by that in Cavell.

43. Ibid., p. 209.

44. Max Weber, "Politik als Beruf," *Gesammelte Politische Schriften,* dritte Auflage (Tübingen: Mohr, 1971), p. 505. English translation in *From Max Weber,* ed. H. Gerth and C. W. Mills (New York: Oxford, 1947).

45. See my articles, "Weber and Freud: Vocation and Self-Acknowledgment," *Canadian Journal of Sociology* 10 (4): 391–408 and "Entitlement and Legitimacy: Weber and Lenin on the Problems of Leadership," in *Constitutional Democracy,* pp. 153–183.

46. Cavell, *The Claim of Reason,* p. 15.

47. St. Augustine, *Confessions.*

48. I am drawing here on most of Foucault's texts, especially *Les mots et les choses* (Paris: Gallimard, 1966); *L'archéologie du savoir* (Paris: Gallimard, 1969): *Surveiller et punir* (Paris: Gallimard, 1975); the essays in *Language, Counter-memory, Practice* (New York: Random House, 1965); *La naissance de la clinique* (Paris: Presses Universitaires de France, 1963). I have been aided by the discussion in Gilles Deleuze, *Foucault* (Paris: Editions de Minuit, 1986), as well as in conversations with William Connolly and Tom Keenan.

49. See Foucault, *Les mots et les choses,* chaps. 4–6.

50. G. W. F. Hegel, *The Philosophy of Right* (Oxford: Oxford University Press, 1966), p. 84.

51. Interestingly, from Foucault's point of view it would be wrong to read Marx (but perhaps not Locke!) as saying that labor is the human essence. Such a reading comes from the desire to find a theological reading of Marx, presumably for the purpose of avoiding the difficulties that his doctrine and the nineteenth-century notion of man present.

52. The passage in Hegel is of course in the "Lordship and Bondage Section" of the *Phenomenology of Mind* (London: Allen and Un-

win, 1966), pp. 243 ff, as well as in sections 54 ff of the *Philosophy of Right*. See A. Kojève, *Introduction à la lecture de Hegel* (Paris: Gallimard, 1947) as well as George Kelly's incisive criticism in "Notes on Lordship and Bondage" in *Hegel*, ed. A. MacIntyre (Notre Dame, Ind.: University of Notre Dame Press, 1976). The importance of Kojève's interpretation of a generation of French existential Marxists has been well laid out by Raymond Aron in *History and the Dialectic of Violence* (Oxford: Basil Blackwell, 1975).

53. See the discussion in Strong, *Friedrich Nietzsche and the Transfiguration of Politics*, pp. 10–19, 258–259, and chapter 9. There are, I have discovered not to my surprise, similar considerations in Cavell, *Claim of Reason*, pp. 467–468 and some of my language in rewriting has been influenced by his.

54. This is in "What is an Author?" in *The Foucault Reader*, ed. Paul Rabinow (New York: Pantheon, 1984).

55. See my "Nihilism and Political Theory," in *What Should Political Theory be Now?*

56. See Jean-Luc Nancy, *L'oubli de la philosophie* (Paris: Editions de Minuit, 1986).

57. Michel Foucault, "The History of Sexuality," in *Power/Knowledge*, ed. Colin Gordon (New York: Pantheon, 1980).

58. See C. B. Macpherson, *The Political Theory of Possessive Individualism* (New York: Oxford University Press, 1962); Peter Laslett, "Introduction," to John Locke, *Two Treatises on Government* (New York: Mentor, 1972); Richard Ashcraft, *Locke and Revolutionary Politics* (Princeton, N.J.: Princeton University Press, 1986).

59. J. J. Rousseau, *The First and Second Discourses and Essay on the Origin of Languages*, ed. and trans. by Victor Gourevitch (New York: Harper and Row, 1986), p. 170.

60. Ibid., p. 245.

61. Ibid., p. 246. See the discussion of this passage in Cavell, *Claim of Reason*, p. 466.

62. Rousseau, *First and Second Discourses*, p. 197.

63. Ibid., pp. 198–199.

64. See the range of literature that stretches from David Riesman et al., *The Lonely Crowd* to Robert Bellah et al., *Habits of the Heart*. During the 1960s, much political science literature celebrated this fact and proclaimed, in the words of Robert Lane, that "a touch of anomie" was necessary for "democracy" to "work." See Robert Lane, *Political Ideology* (Glencoe, Ill.: Free Press, 1962).

65. See my "On Bottled Spiders and Intelligencers: Machiavelli and Elizabethan Statecraft," in *The Artist and Political Vision*, ed. Benjamin Barber and Michael McGrath (New Brunswick, N.J.: Transaction Press, 1982).

66. Richard Rorty, *Philosophy and the Mirror of Nature* (Princeton, N.J.: Princeton University Press, 1979).

67. Cavell, *Claim of Reason,* p. 473.

68. Gunnell, *Political Theory.*

69. On the pianissimo of the private, see Max Weber, "Science as a Vocation" in *From Max Weber,* ed. Gerth and Mills, p. 155.

70. Claude Lévi-Strauss, *The Scope of Anthropology* (London: Cape, 1967), pp. 38–39.

2. THE PROMISE AND LURE OF AESTHETICS

1. Among the best discussions are Alexander Nehamas, "Plato on Imitation and Poetry in Republic X" in *Plato and the Arts,* ed. Julius Moravsic (Oxford: Oxford University Press, 1980) and Iris Murdoch, *The Fire and the Sun: Why Plato Banished the Artists* (Oxford: Clarendon, 1977).

2. *Encyclopedie,* "Genève," vol. 7 nouvelle impression en fasicule (Stuttgart: Froman, 1966), p. 577. Allan Bloom in *Politics and the Arts* (Glencoe, Ill.: Free Press, 1960) translates "*sagesse*" as "prudence" and "*politesse*" as "urbanity."

3. See the brilliant discussion by Jean-Christophe Agnew, *Worlds Apart* (Cambridge: Cambridge University Press, 1986), p. xi and *passim.*

4. Jean-Pierre Vernant and Pierre Vidal-Naquet, *Mythe et tragédie en grèce ancienne* (Paris: Maspéro, 1973), pp. 15, 25.

5. Allan Bloom affects briefly to believe this (*Politics and the Arts,* pp. xv–xvi). Rousseau explains his writing of dramas in the "Preface" to *Narcisse, Oeuvres Complets,* vol. 2 (Paris: Gallimard, 1959), pp. 959–974. See the informative presentation in Maurice Cranston, *Jean-Jacques Rousseau* (New York: W. W. Norton, 1983).

6. See Rousseau, *Lettre à M. D'Alembert sur les spectacles,* ed. M. Fuchs (Paris: Droz, 1948), pp. 90 ff. It is perhaps worth noting that political leaders have sometimes sought severely to regulate theater and that theater has never been able to accept this restriction. This is true both in China and the USSR; perhaps the closest to success was under Louis XIV. But there was not only a Molière for each Racine; even Racine had his subversions. See Lucien Goldmann, *Le dieu caché* (Paris: Gallimard, 1956).

7. Agnew, *Worlds Apart,* p. xiii.

8. Aristotle, *Poetics,* 1449b 24, 31, 36; 1450a 15–23, 38–39; 1450b 2–3.

9. See here Richard Wollheim, *Painting as an Art* (London: Thames and Hudson, 1987), chap. 2.

10. Michael Goldman, *The Actor's Freedom: Towards a Theory of Drama* (New York: Viking, 1965), p. 160; cf. pp. 3f.

11. See here Stanley Cavell, *The World Viewed: Reflections on the Ontology of Cinema* (New York: Viking, 1971).

12. See the classic essay by Michael Fried, "Art and Objecthood," *Artforum* 5, no. 10 (1967): 12–28.

13. The phrase is from the "General Confession" in the *Book of Common Prayer.*

14. See the discussion of Rousseau in chapter 1.

15. Thus Richard Wollheim, an aesthetician, writes of personhood in *The Thread of Life* (Cambridge, Mass.: Harvard University Press, 1984) as "the leading of a life."

16. We live *in* the world, and *on* the stage.

17. See Camus's development of this theme at the end of *The Rebel.*

18. Calvin, *Institutions de la religion chrétienne,* ed. Baum, Cunitz, and Reuss, *Opera omnia* (Brunswic, 1965), Volume 3–4, tome I, pp. 488, 496.

19. See Vernant, *Mythe et tragédie,* pp. 13–17.

20. Goldman, *Actor's Freedom,* pp. 13–17.

21. Aristotle, *Problemata,* vol. VII of *Works in English,* trans. W. D. Ross (Oxford: Clarendon, 1927), xix, 48.18.

22. See my discussion of the aesthetic roots of this move in "Nietzsche's Political Aesthetics," in *Towards New Seas.*

23. See inter alia, Stanley Fish, "Literature in the Reader: Affective Stylistics," *New Literary History* (Autumn 1970): 123–162, and Cavell, "A Matter of Meaning It," in *Must We Mean What We Say?* pp. 213–217.

24. Aristotle, *Poetics,* 1450b 24ff.

25. See Hegel's comments in *Aesthetics,* vol. II, p. 1217. The above paragraph is strongly influenced by Cavell, *The World Viewed.*

26. See Benjamin Barber, "Rousseau and Brecht," in *The Artist and Political Vision,* ed. B. Barber and M. J. McGrath.

27. Rousseau, *Lettre à d'Alembert,* pp. 32, 69.

28. A production of *The Caucasian Chalk Circle* at the 1975 Edinburgh Festival by the Georgian national company tends to make me think that it can be realized.

29. See the similar reflections in Jean-Louis Barrault, *Réflexions sur le théâtre* (Paris: Vautrin, 1949), pp. 130–132. This essay is a reflection on Diderot's *Paradoxe sur le comédien.*

30. See here the seminal essay by Helene Keyssar, "I love you. Who are you? The Strategy of Drama in Recognition Scenes," *Publication of the Modern Language Association,* 97, 2 (March 1977): 297–306, and Goldman, *Actor's Freedom,* pp. 29–34.

31. Cavell, *The World Viewed,* p. 64.

32. See here David Cole, *The Theatrical Event* (Middletown, Conn.: Wesleyan University Press, 1975), pp. 12–53, for a comparison of the actor and shaman, and also Goldman, *Actor's Freedom,* esp. pp. 26–29, on the actor as ghost. See the critique of Goldman in Keyssar, "Strategy of Recognition Scenes."

33. I have explored this topic more fully in "Nietzsche's Political Aesthetics," cited above and in my forthcoming *The Development of Aesthetic Politics, 1890–1933.*

34. See the discussion in Cavell, *Must We Mean What We Say?* last chapter.

35. See here my review of Ernest Gellner, *Contemporary Thought and Politics* (London: Routledge and Kegan Paul, 1974) in *Theory and Society* 1, 4, (1974): 503–505.

36. On Greece, see here Vernant, *Mythe et tragédie,* esp. pp. 41–76; Roger Sales, "Achilles and Heroic Values," *Arion* 2, 3, (Autumn, 1963): 46–58; and Noah Greenberg, "Socrates' Choice in the *Crito,*" *Harvard Studies in Classical Philology* 70 (1965): 46–82. Perhaps the beginning of this comes in *The Epic of Gilgamesh,* when the hero, recognizing his equality with Enkidu, bonds together with him to undertake deeds for which they will be remembered (i.e., to achieve immortality in the only way humans can, and to attack or at least ignore the gods). The polis has an origin in Middle Eastern townships according to Patricia Springborg, *Royal Persons* (forthcoming).

37. On the question of all drama, see Helene Keyssar, "Theater Games, Language Games and *Endgame,*" *Theatre Journal* 31, 2 (May 1979): 221–238.

38. Aristotle, *Poetics,* 1452a 20.

39. This leads him into some troubles, as Thomas Gould, "The Innocence of Oedipus," *Arion* 4, 3 (Autumn 1965): 363–368 has pointed out.

40. This is a rejection of some readings of *hamartia* (the so-called "tragic flaw") as well as of the idea that the Greeks understood "acting freely (*hekon*)" in the sense that we do. On both points, see Vernant, *Mythe et tragédie,* pp. 49–71.

41. See F. Nietzsche, *The Gay Science* (New York: Random House, 1974), #340, and my *Friedrich Nietzsche and the Politics of Transfiguration,* chapter 9, for a full discussion.

42. See the discussion of *pharmakon* in J. Derrida, "Plato's Pharmacy," *Disseminations* (Chicago: University of Chicago Press, 1981).

43. Goldman, *Actor's Freedom,* pp. 27–28.

44. This is why melodrama pushes at the limits of drama.

45. Compare here Gareth Matthews, "Bodily Motions and Religious Feelings," *Canadian Journal of Philosophy* 1, 1 (1971): 75–86.

46. J. L. Austin, "Pretending," *Philosophical Papers*, 2d ed. (Oxford: Clarendon, 1970), p. 256.

47. There are limits to this. See the discussion in André Green, *Un oeil en trop* (Paris: Editions de minuit, 1969) of a performance of Pirandello's *Enrico Quattro*.

48. Jean-Louis Barrault, *Nouvelles reflexions sur le théâtre* (Paris: Flammarion, 1959), p. 59.

49. It is interesting to note that those characteristics that cannot be put on stage are very close to those that Peter Winch identifies as the universally human at the end of his "Understanding a Primitive Society," *American Philosophical Quarterly* 1 (October 1964): 307–324.

50. Stanley Fish, *Self-Consuming Artifacts* (Berkeley and Los Angeles: University of California Press, 1972), p. 425.

51. Friedrich Nietzsche, *Die Geburt der Tragödie aus dem Geist der Musik*, #8, in *Werke Kritische Gesammtausgabe* III (Berlin: Gruyter, 1969), p. 55 (Nietzsche's italics; my translation).

52. Nietzsche does *not* use that special German word *Aufhebung*.

53. Hegel had moved towards this understanding when he pointed out that the chorus was a "background" on which "there arise individual characters who play an active role." See *Aesthetics*, vol. I, p. 192 and vol. II, p. 16.

54. Compare Goldman, *Actor's Freedom*, p. 16.

55. See the discussion in Fish, *Self-Consuming Artifacts*, pp. 43–77.

56. Election-day sermons formed one of the foci of New England public life. See *The Wall and the Garden*, ed. A. W. Plumstead (Minneapolis: University of Minnesota Press, 1968).

57. M. Merleau-Ponty, *La prose du monde* (Paris: Gallimard, 1969), p. 96.

58. Clifford Geertz, "Ideology as a Cultural System," in *Interpretation of Cultures*, p. 211. Geertz goes on to discuss explicitly on p. 219 the question of cultural strain.

59. See here Nehamas, *Nietzsche: Life as Literature* and my "Nietzsche's Aesthetic Politics," in *Towards New Seas*.

60. See the discussion in my "The Artistic Foundations of Political Space," in *Structure, Consciousness and History*, ed. R. Brown and S. Lyman (Cambridge: Cambridge University Press, 1977).

61. For Greek times, see Vernant, *Mythe et tragédie*, p. 39; for Elizabethan times, see my "On Bottled Spiders and Intelligencers," pp. 191–220. See the discussion by Lincoln of the relation of the past to the American Revolution in "Speech to the Young Man's Lyceum," in *Complete Works*, I (New Brunswick, N.J.: Rutgers University Press, 1953).

62. See Martin Ostwald, *Nomos and the Beginnings of Athenian Democracy* (Oxford: Clarendon, 1968), esp. pp. 20 ff.

63. *Crito*, 50a ff.

64. Rousseau, *Lettre à d'Alembert,* pp. 24–30.

65. A. Zolberg, "Moments of Madness," *Politics and Society* 2, 2 (Winter 1972): 183–207. His analysis draws its inspiration from Hannah Arendt, *On Revolution* (New York: Viking, 1963). See also Kenneth Benne, "The Uses of Fraternity," *Daedalus* (Summer 1957).

66. I am conscious of having learned much from S. Cavell, "The Avoidance of Love," in *Must We Mean What We Say?* pp. 267–356, and Henry Jaffa's chapter in Allan Bloom, *Shakespeare's Politics* (New York: Basic Books, 1964).

67. Goldman, *Actor's Freedom,* 16 f.

68. Some portions of Henry VIII may have been written by Shakespeare.

3. SCIENCE AND POLITICAL THEORY AS ACTIVITIES

1. This is one of the deep messages of Hannah Arendt, *Eichmann in Jerusalem* (New York: Viking, 1974). She argues there (p. 279) that only death can redeem the human being from that sentence: it is her most Heideggerian book and, properly, she is only Heideggerian in extreme situations.

2. See Wolin, "Politics as a Vocation."

3. David Hume, "That Politics May be Reduced to a Science," *Political Essays* (Indianapolis: Bobbs Merrill, 1953), pp. 12–23 and especially p. 18: "Legislators, therefore, ought not to trust the future government of a state entirely to chance, but ought to provide a system of laws to regulate the administration of public affairs to the latest posterity. Effects will always correspond to causes. . . ."

4. G. W. F. Hegel, *The Phenomenology of Mind,* Preface.

5. Max Weber, *Economy and Society,* vol. I (Berkeley: University of California Press, 1978), pp. 4 ff. See my "Weber and Lenin: Problems of Entitlement and Legitimacy," in *Constitutional Democracy,* ed. F. Eidlin.

6. Alasdair MacIntyre, "Is a Science of Comparative Politics Possible?" *Against the Self-Images of the Age,* esp. pp. 275–276, and *After Virtue.* On the moral quality of narrative see Hayden White, "On Narrative," in *On Narrative,* ed. W. J. T. Mitchell, p. 23.

7. See for instance those posited by Peter Winch, "Understanding a Primitive Society," *American Philosophical Quarterly* 1 (October 1964): 307–324, or those in Melford Spiro, "Cultural Relativism and

the Future of Anthropology," *Cultural Anthropology* 1, 3 (August 1986): 259–286.

8. See Geertz, *Interpretation of Cultures,* pp. 208–213.

9. But see Charles Taylor, *The Explanation of Behavior* (London: Routledge & Kegan Paul, 1964), p. 36 f.

10. See the discussion in Spiro, "Cultural Relativism," esp. pp. 273 ff, and that by Steven Lukes, "Relativism in Its Place," *Rationality and Relativism,* ed. M. Hollis and S. Lukes (Oxford: Basil Blackwell, 1982).

11. See Richard Taylor, *Action and Purpose* (Englewood Cliffs, N.J.: Prentice Hall, 1966), pp. 104 ff.

12. Louis Althusser, *Lire le Capital,* vol. I (Paris: Maspéro, 1968), p. 74 (my translation and interpolations).

13. See Stanley Cavell, *The Senses of Walden* (New York: Viking, 1972), pp. 103–104.

14. Cavell, *Must We Mean What We Say?* p. 64.

15. See Georg Simmel, "What is Society?" in *Philosophy of the Social Sciences,* ed. Maurice Natanson (New York: Random House, 1963).

16. Kant, *The Critique of Judgment* (Indianapolis: Library of Liberal Arts, 1968), p. 84.

17. See the texts collected in Natanson, ed., *Philosophy of the Social Sciences* and in Leonard Krimerman, ed., *Philosophy of the Social Sciences* (New York: Appleton, Century, Crofts, 1969).

18. Cavell, *The Claim of Reason,* pp. 96–100. A good deal of weight is placed here on "ordinarily." I wish merely to indicate by this that it is the quality of experience to be known. For an examination of this in Nietzsche, see my *Friedrich Nietzsche and the Politics of Transfiguration,* chapter 10. See a similar analysis in Wilfrid Sellars, *Science, Perception and Reality* (London: Routledge & Kegan Paul, 1963), pp. 321–322, 328.

19. Peter Winch, who inherits this tradition even if he reads it (wrongly, I think) into Wittgenstein, makes this mistake. See the discussion in Pitkin, *Wittgenstein and Justice.*

20. Wittgenstein, *Philosophical Investigations* (New York: Macmillan, 1958), par. 644. See the discussion in Austin, "Pretending," in *Philosophical Papers.*

21. Wittgenstein, *Philosophical Investigations,* par. 641.

22. See Cavell, *Must We Mean What We Say?* p. 25.

28. See similar comments by Max Weber on the "pestilence of methodology" in *Critique of Stammler,* trans. and ed. Guy Oakes (New York: Free Press, 1977).

24. T. S. Kuhn, "Reflections on My Critics," *Criticism and the*

Growth of Knowledge, ed. I. Lakatos and A. Musgrave (Cambridge: Cambridge University Press, 1970), p. 237.

25. See Austin, *Philosophical Papers,* p. 175.

26. For an elaborate discussion of the relationship between the elements of an understanding and that which is understood, see Althusser, *Lire le Capital,* sections 16 and 17.

27. Alexandre Koyré, *Metaphysics and Measurement* (Cambridge, Mass.: Harvard University Press, 1968).

28. Stephen Toulmin, *Foresight and Understanding* (Bloomington, Ind.: Indiana University Press, 1961), p. 95. See the discussion of these claims in Hollis and Lukes, eds., *Rationality and Relativism.*

29. Nelson Goodman, "Seven Structures Against Similarity," in *Experience and Theory,* ed. L. Foster and J. W. Swanson (Amherst, Mass.: University of Massachusetts Press, 1970), pp. 22 f.

30. See Bishop Berkeley, "An essay towards a new theory of vision," *Works,* I (Oxford: Oxford University Press, 1948), p. 190; see also H. A. Pritchard, "The Sense-Datum Fallacy," *Aristotelian Society Supplementary Volume,* VII (London: Routledge, 1938).

31. See Cavell, *Must We Mean What We Say?* pp. 15–18; see M. Scriven, "Definitions, Explanations and Theories," *Minnesota Studies in the Philosophy of Science,* vol. II, ed. E. H. Feigl, M. Scriven, G. Maxwell (Minneapolis: University of Minnesota Press, 1958); see Donald Davidson, "On the Very Idea of a Conceptual Scheme," in *Post-Analytical Philosophy,* ed. John Rajchman and Cornel West (New York: Columbia University Press, 1985), esp. p. 143.

32. W. V. O. Quine, *Ontological Relativity* (New York: Columbia University Press, 1969), p. 48.

33. Maurice Merleau-Ponty, *The Structure of Behavior* (Boston: Beacon, 1967), pp. 7–51.

34. See Strong, *Friedrich Nietzsche and the Politics of Transfiguration,* chapter 8.

35. See S. Shapin and S. Schaffer, *Leviathan and Airpump: Hobbes, Boyle and the Experimental Life* (Princeton, N.J.: Princeton University Press, 1985), esp. p. 81.

36. Sellars, *Science, Perception and Reality,* pp. 147–148.

37. This argument is made in forcible detail in Cavell, *Must We Mean What We Say?* chap. 1; see G. E. Moore, "Wittgenstein's Lectures in 1930–31, *Mind* 43 (1934): 7–15.

38. Sellars, *Science, Perception and Reality,* pp. 39–40.

39. See Wittgenstein, *Philosophical Investigations*; Wittgenstein, *On Certainty;* Pitkin, *Wittgenstein and Justice.*

40. This is an extension of the notion of "essentially contested concepts" advanced by W. B. Gallie in *Philosophy and the Historical*

Understanding (New York: Schocken, 1968), pp. 157–191, and extended by William Connolly in *The Terms of Political Discourse.*

41. See F. Waismann, "Verifiability," in *Logic and Language,* ed. A. Flew (New York: Anchor, 1977), pp. 308–319.

42. See Thomas S. Kuhn, *The Essential Tension* (Chicago: University of Chicago Press, 1977), pp. 305 ff. It is worth realizing that Kuhn has a strong predilection for what he calls normal science: he is precisely not suggesting that a black swan revolutionize the taxonomy of waterfowl. As to possible questions about the limits to this procedure, see Cavell, *The Claim of Reason.*

43. This link is approvingly drawn in Paul Feyerabend, "Against Method: Outline of an Anarchistic Theory of Knowledge," in *Minnesota Studies in the Philosophy of Science,* IV, ed. M. Radner and W. S. Winokur (Minneapolis: University of Minnesota Press, 1970), p. 109.

44. Merleau-Ponty, *The Structure of Behavior,* p. 102.

45. Sellars, *Science, Perception and Reality,* p. 39.

46. See the polemical but worthwhile discussion in Barry Hindess, *Philosophy and Methodology in the Social Sciences* (New York: Harvester Press, 1977), esp. Introduction and chapter 4. See Ludwig Fleck, *The Genesis and Development of a Scientific Fact* (1935; Chicago: University of Chicago Press, 1979), pp. 92 and 177.

47. See Sellars, *Science, Perception and Reality,* pp. 310–332; Toulmin, *Foresight and Understanding*; R. G. Collingwood, *An Essay on Metaphysics;* and Matthews, "Bodily Motions and Religious Feelings."

48. See Donald Davidson, "On The Very Idea of a Conceptual System." I take this to be a formal version of Lukes' argument in Hollis and Lukes, *Rationality and Relativism.*

49. Ian Hacking, "The Accumulation of Styles of Scientific Reasoning," in *Kant oder Hegel,* ed. Dieter Henrich (Stuttgart: Klett-Cotta, 1983), pp. 453–465. See also Michel Foucault, *L'archéologie du savoir.*

50. See Cavell, *The Senses of Walden,* pp. 93–94, 104–105. In philosophy of science literature, see F. Waissman, "Verifiability," in *Logic and Language,* ed. A. Flew, pp. 137 ff; P. Feyerabend, "Explanation, Reduction and Empiricism," in *Minnesota Studies in the Philosophy of Science,* vol. III, ed. H. Feigl and G. Maxwell (Minneapolis: University of Minnesota Press, 1962), p. 29; W. Heisenberg, *Physics and Beyond* (New York: Harper, 1972). For what appears to be a complaint about this, see P. Achinstein, *Law and Explanation* (Oxford: Oxford University Press, 1971) and for a defense, N. R. Hanson, *Patterns of Discovery* (Cambridge: Cambridge University Press, 1948), pp. 136–149, esp. 141.

51. See M. Oakeshott, "The Voice of Poetry in the Experience of Mankind" in *Rationalism in Politics* and his *On Human Conduct;*

Waismann, "Verifiability"; Aristotelian Society, ed. "Are Necessary Truths Truths by Convention," *Supplementary Volume XXI,* (London: Routledge, 1947), pp. 78–133, esp. 100–103; W. V. O. Quine, "Meaning and Translation," in *On Translation,* ed. R. Brouwer (Cambridge, Mass., 1959), p. 165; Quine, *Ontological Relativity.*

52. See, e.g., A. Schutz, *Collected Papers,* vol. I, (The Hague: Nijhoff), pp. 3–47.

53. Cf. Quine, "Meaning and Translation," p. 168; see Clifford Geertz, "'From the Native's Point of View': On the Nature of Anthropological Understanding," *Meaning in Anthropology,* ed. K. H. Basso and H. A. Selby (Albuquerque: University of New Mexico Press, 1976), pp. 236–237, for a flirtation with hermeneutics; see the discussion of Winch in Pitkin, *Wittgenstein and Justice.*

54. For an analysis of this notion of person, see my *Friedrich Nietzsche and the Politics of Transfiguration,* pp. 294–309, and (I think) Parfit, *Reasons and Persons.* See the Bart Schultz, "Persons, Selves and Utilitarianism," pp. 744–745.

55. Israel Scheffler, *Science and Subjectivity,* (Englewood, N.J.: Prentice Hall, 1967), p. 19; see also C. R. Kordig, "The Theory-Ladenness of Observations," *Review of Metaphysics* 24, 3 (March 1971): 448–484, esp. 454, 468.

56. Kuhn, "Reflections on My Critics," pp. 264–265.

57. Feyerabend, "Against Method," p. 80. He goes on to talk unnecessarily in favor of the inclusion of "irrational elements" into science. To me this seems to accept the notion of rationality that he claims to be opposing. It is more meaningful to argue about the notion of rationality.

58. See here the discussion by Hayden White in *Metahistory* (Baltimore: Johns Hopkins Press, 1973) with his analysis of the tendency of nineteenth-century thought to slide towards Romance, Tragedy, or Comedy. White is concerned with rhetorical styles; I am concerned with communities of discourse.

59. T. S. Kuhn, "Notes on Lakatos," *Boston Studies in the Philosophy of Science,* vol. VIII, ed. R. Buck and R. Cohen (Dordrecht: Reidel, 1971), p. 144.

60. Alan Blum, *Theorizing* (London: Gower, 1974), p. 182.

61. Sellars, *Science, Perception and Reality.*

62. See Strong, *Friedrich Nietzsche and the Politics of Transfiguration,* chap. 7.

63. Hanson, *Patterns of Discovery,* pp. 6–8.

64. See Kordig, "The Theory-Ladenness of Observations."

65. I think this is what Wittgenstein means by "often extremely general facts of nature"; see *Philosophical Investigations,* p. 56.

66. See, e.g., Gerald Doppelt, "Kuhn's Epistemological Relativ-

ism: An Interpretation and a Defense," *Inquiry* 21 (1978): 33–86; Richard J. Bernstein, *Beyond Objectivism and Relativity* (Oxford: Oxford University Press, 1983), esp. part II.

67. The best starting point is the classic article by C. G. Hempel and Paul Oppenheim, "Studies in the Logic of Explanation," *Philosophy of Science* 15 (1948): 135–175. See the critique by M. Scriven, "Explanations, Predictions and Laws," in *Minnesota Studies in the Philosophy of Science* III, ed. Feigl and Maxwell, pp. 170–230.

68. Sellars, *Science, Perception and Reality,* p. 124; see p. 328.

69. Paul Feyerabend, "Consolations for the Specialist," in *Criticism and the Growth of Knowledge,* ed. I. Lakatos and R. Musgrave (Cambridge: Cambridge University Press, 1970), p. 221.

70. Wittgenstein, *Philosophical Investigations,* p. 195; see Hanson, *Patterns of Discovery,* pp. 13–14.

71. Wittgenstein, *Philosophical Investigations,* p. 212.

72. See Strong, *Friedrich Nietzsche and the Politics of Transfiguration,* chapter 2.

73. I am conscious of having been prompted here by the thoughts in Cavell, *The Claim of Reason,* pp. 370–372.

74. Wittgenstein, *Philosophical Investigations,* p. 226 (italics added).

75. Wittgenstein, *On Certainty,* #298.

76. Sellars, *Science, Perception and Reality,* p. 40.

77. Wittgenstein, *On Certainty,* #665. This is the point of the title essay in Cavell's, *Must We Mean What We Say?*

78. See Wittgenstein, *On Certainty,* #95–99; Collingwood, *An Essay on Metaphysics;* S. Toulmin, "Conceptual Revolution in Science," in *Boston Studies in the Philosophy of Science,* vol. III.

79. I. Lakatos and R. Musgrave, eds., *Criticism and the Growth of Knowledge.*

80. For examples, see I. Lakatos, "History of Science and Its Rational Reconstruction," in *Boston Studies in the Philosophy of Science,* vol. VIII, ed. Buck and Cohen, pp. 91–136; see Kuhn, "Reflections on My Critics," pp. 262–264.

81. Fleck, *Genesis and Development of a Scientific Fact,* p. 141. Fleck's book is a study of the genesis and development of syphilis as a disease; it was highly influential on Kuhn in the writing of his *The Structure of Scientific Revolutions.* On the notion of a style see also the work by Hacking, "The Accumulation of Styles of Scientific Reasoning."

82. Cavell, *Must We Mean What We Say?* p. 39.

83. As does Feyerabend, "Against Method," p. 80; see *contra* the Nietzsche/Foucault links drawn by Gillian Rose in *The Dialectic of Nihilism* (Oxford: Basil Blackwell, 1984).

84. See my discussion of Max Weber, in "Weber and Lenin: Problems of Entitlement and Legitimacy."

85. There is no need here to be as strong as Fleck, when he claims (*Genesis and Development*, p. 139) that between two far removed thought-styles "words cannot be translated and concepts have nothing in common. . . ." For more discussion on this, see the last chapter.

86. Maurice Merleau-Ponty, *Sense and Non-Sense* (Evanston, Ill.: Northwestern University Press, 1964), p. 91.

87. See F. Manuel, *A Portrait of Isaac Newton* (Cambridge, Mass.: Harvard University Press, 1964); J. M. Keynes, "Newton the Man," in *Essays in Biography* (New York: Norton, 1963).

88. See here S. Lakoff, "The Third Culture: Science in Social Thought," in *Knowledge and Power: Essays on Science and Government* (New York: Free Press, 1966).

89. Here I draw heavily on Shapin and Schaffer, *Leviathan and the Airpump: Hobbes, Boyle and the Experimental Life.*

90. Ibid., p. 80.

91. See the discussion of the sociology and politics of the esoteric and exoteric circles of knowledge and of their relation to each other in Fleck, *Genesis and Development,* pp. 105 ff.

92. Shapin and Schaffer, *Leviathan and Airpump,* p. 60.

93. See Alasdair MacIntyre, "Is a Science of Comparative Politics Possible?" in *Against the Self-Images of the Age.*

94. Feyerabend, "Consolations for the Specialist," p. 209.

95. "Can you," Max Weber asks, "stand to see your results constantly superceded?" See "Science as a Vocation" in *From Max Weber,* ed. H. Gerth and C. W. Mills.

96. Donald W. Fisbe and Richard A. Shweder, eds., *Metatheory in the Social Sciences* (Chicago: University of Chicago Press, 1986).

97. Robert Dahl, *A Preface to Democratic Theory* (Englewood Cliffs, N.J.: Prentice Hall, 1963), pp. 138–139.

98. See Steven Erie, *Rainbow's End* (Berkeley and Los Angeles: University of California Press, 1987) for an argument that casts considerable doubt on the received wisdom that such assimilation was the natural lot of the Irish.

99. See H. Kariel, *Open Systems* (Notre Dame, Ind.: University of Notre Dame Press, 1969), pp. 69–75.

100. See Pocock, *Politics, Language and Time* (Chicago: University of Chicago Press, 1986).

101. Feyerabend, "Against Method," p. 91.

102. Feyerabend, "Consolations for the Specialist," p. 210.

103. See G. Deleuze and F. Guattari, *L'antioedipe* (Paris: Editions de Minuit, 1972) for a defense of serious madness as a political endeavor.

104. See S. S. Wolin, *Politics and Vision* (Boston: Little, Brown, 1961), chap. 10; Pitkin, *Wittgenstein and Justice.*

4. POLITICAL THEORY AND HISTORY

1. T. D. Weldon, *The Vocabulary of Politics* (Baltimore: Penguin Books, 1953).
2. Thomas Hobbes, *Leviathan* (Oxford: Basil Blackwell, 1951), chapter 2.
3. Wittgenstein, *Philosophical Investigations,* #133, 128.
4. See Cavell, *The Claim of Reason,* pp. 33–34.
5. Isaiah Berlin, *Four Essays on Liberty* (Oxford: Oxford University Press, 1969), p. 168.
6. John Rawls, "Justice as Fairness: Political Not Metaphysical," *Philosophy and Public Affairs* 15, 3 (Spring 1985): 226.
7. John Rawls, *A Theory of Justice* (Cambridge, Mass.: Harvard University Press, 1971), pp. 12, 136–142.
8. This is not completely true since the Rawlsian chooser apparently knows a certain amount of Keynesian economics. See *A Theory of Justice,* pp. 265 ff.
9. Judith Shklar argues that despotism is rule based on the body (*Montesquieu* [Oxford: Oxford University Press, 1987], p. 85). If so, the need to avoid despotism has driven Rawls to construct a person without physiology.
10. Robert Nozick, *Anarchy, State, Utopia* (New York: Basic Books, 1974). I am indebted here to Benjamin R. Barber, *The Conquest of Politics: Liberal Philosophy in Democratic Times* (Princeton, N.J.: Princeton University Press, 1988).
11. Hannah Arendt, *The Human Condition* (Garden City, N.Y.: Anchor, 1958).
12. Max Weber, *Economy and Society,* p. 961; cf. p. 954.
13. Max Weber, "Parliament und Regierung im neugeordneten Deutschland," *Gesammelte Politische Schriften* (Tübingen: Mohr, 1971), pp. 329n1, 351 (translation in *Economy and Society,* pp. 1399, 1417).
14. Stephen Toulmin and June Goodfield, *The Fabric of the Heavens* (London: Hutchinson, 1961).
15. Until recently politics was not (truly) available to women. This fact is of great importance in understanding what politics has meant and might mean. It is at the core of the most important of the feminist developments of political thought.
16. I take Allan Bloom to share this position. See his commentary to his edition of the *Republic* (New York: Basic Books, 1968).
17. See Margaret Leslie, "In Defense of Anachronism," *Political Studies* 18, 4 (1970): 433–447. See also the discussion of this essay in J. Peter Euben's forthcoming book from Cornell University Press on Greek tragedy, as well as his "Introduction" to *Greek Tragedy and*

Political Theory (Berkeley: University of California Press, 1986). This position is opposed to the one advanced by Stephen Holmes, "Aristippus in and out of Athens," *American Political Science Review* 73, 1 (March 1979): 113–128.

18. In the *Republic*, the theoretical attitude is given first exposition in a discussion of astronomy. As Toulmin and Goodfield make clear in *Fabric of the Heavens*, this is no historical accident.

19. Merleau-Ponty, *The Structure of Behavior*, p. 90.

20. See the work of W. V. O. Quine for the most radical statement of this position. For a more limited version, see Connolly, *Terms of Political Discourse*.

21. For a complete analysis of this point see my *Friedrich Nietzsche and the Politics of Transfiguration*, pp. 294–309.

22. Maurice Merleau-Ponty, *La phénomenologie de la perception* (Paris: Gallimard, 1945), p. 77.

23. Ibid., p. 454.

24. Stanley Cavell suggests it in *The World Viewed*, p. 157.

25. See here J. Searle, *Speech Acts* (Cambridge: Cambridge University Press, 1970); A. MacIntyre, *Against the Self-Images of the Age.*

26. Raymond Aron, "Note sur la structure en sciences politiques," cited in Jean Viet, *Les methodes structuralistes dans les sciences sociales* (Paris: Mouton, 1967), p. 195.

27. See the work of Michael Scriven, "Definitions, Explanations, and Theories" and "Explanations, Predictions, and Laws"; see George Kateb, *Political Theory: Its Nature and Uses* (New York: St. Martin's Press, 1968).

28. Friedrich Nietzsche, *Beyond Good and Evil* (New York: Vintage, 1967), par. 39. One thinks here of Max Weber who in response to a question of why he learned so much answered: "I want to see how much I can bear." For a discussion of this point in relation to madness, see my "Oedipus as Hero: Family and Family Metaphors in Nietzsche," *boundary 2: a journal of post-modern literature* (Spring/Fall 1981): 311–336.

29. Charles Taylor, "Neutrality in Political Science," in *Philosophical Papers* vol. 2; William Connolly, *Appearance and Reality in Politics* (Cambridge: Cambridge University Press, 1981).

30. Merleau-Ponty, *La phénomenologie de la perception*, p. 78. See also Paul Ricoeur, *Husserl: An Analysis of his Phenomenology* (Evanston, Ill.: Northwestern University Press, 1967), p. 4; Merleau-Ponty, *Structure of Behavior*, p. 125; S. Strasser, *Phénomenologie et sciences de l'homme* (Louvain: Université de Louvain, 1967), pp. 129–146.

31. The phrase was, I believe, given currency in Graham Allison's *Essence of Decision* (Boston: Little, Brown, 1971), p. vi, who explicitly borrowed it from H. D. Price.

32. Max Weber, *The Protestant Ethic and the Spirit of Capitalism* (New York: Scribners, 1958), p. 13.

33. See my "The Deconstruction of the Tradition: The Greeks and Nietzsche," in *Nietzsche and the Rhetoric of Nihilism,* ed. Thomas Darby (Toronto: University of Toronto Press, 1988).

34. See the discussion in Keyssar, "Language Games, Theater Games and *Endgame,*" *Theatre Journal* 31, 1, (May 1979): 221–238.

35. See Karel Kosik, *Le dialectique du concret* (Paris: Maspéro, 1970).

36. See on Newton, Keynes, "Newton the Man," in *Essays in Biography;* W. Heisenberg, *Physics and Beyond* (New York: Harper & Row, 1972); A. Einstein, "Autobiographical Notes" in *Einstein,* vol. II, ed. Paul Schilpp (La Salle, Ill.: Open Court, 1979).

37. Lakatos and Musgrave, *Criticism and the Growth of Knowledge.*

38. The neo-Popperians (Lakatos, Feyerabend) have solved this question by reducing normal science into revolutionary science and discussed a kind of Trotskyite revolution-en-permanence.

39. See Walzer, "On the Role of Symbolism in Political Thought," *Political Science Quarterly.*

40. J. P. Vernant, *Mythe et pensée chez les grecques* (Paris: Maspéro, 1966).

41. Max Weber, *Wissenschaftslehre* (Tübingen: Mohr, 1971), p. 193 (trans. in *The Methodology of the Social Sciences,* ed. E. Shils and R. Finch [Glencoe, Ill.: Free Press, 1949], p. 92).

42. The classic text in Althusser is the chapter on overdetermination in *Pour Marx* (Paris: Maspéro, 1965). See Steven Smith, *Reading Althusser: An Essay on Structural Marxism* (Ithaca, N.Y.: Cornell University Press, 1984) and my review, *Political Theory* 13, 4 (November 1985): 619–622.

43. See my "Nietzsche's Political Aesthetics."

44. Ibid., p. 168.

45. For a good case study, see Ronald L. Meek, *Social Science and the Ignoble Savage* (Cambridge: Cambridge University Press, 1976).

46. Edmund Leach, *Political Systems of Highland Burma* (Boston: Beacon, 1965), pp. 182–195.

47. Claude Lévi-Strauss, *Tristes Tropiques* (New York: Atheneum, 1964), pp. 385–386.

48. Claude Lévi-Strauss, *The Savage Mind* (Chicago: University of Chicago Press, 1966) devotes a chapter to an attack on Sartre; the other text aimed at is probably M. Merleau-Ponty, both *Humanism and Terror* and *The Adventures of the Dialectic.* See the interesting discussion by Aron, *History and the Dialectic of Violence,* pp. 138–158.

49. Compare the following moves to those made by Fish, *Self Consuming Artifacts,* and analyzed in the Appendix to that book.

50. Bruno Latour, "Post-modern? No, simply Amodern! Steps towards an Anthropology of Science," *Studies in History and Philosophy of Science* (forthcoming). My thanks to Professor Latour for making this available to me.

51. Lévi-Strauss, *The Scope of Anthropology,* pp. 52–53.

52. And yet, we must be careful: see F. C. Hood, *The Divine Politics of Thomas Hobbes* (Oxford: Clarendon Press, 1964); see the discussion in my "Thomas Hobbes: The Words and Signs that Authorize" (forthcoming).

53. Norman Jacobson, "Political Science and Political Education," *American Political Science Review* 57, 3 (September 1963): 563.

54. Brice Parain, *Recherches sur la nature et les fonctions du langage* (Paris: Nouvelle revue française, 1942), pp. 21–36. See also the material on Kuhn in the previous chapter as well as the comments by Judith N. Shklar, *A Life of Learning* (American Council of Learned Societies: Occasional Paper No. 9), p. 11.

55. G. W. F. Hegel, *The Philosophy of History* in *The Philosophy of Hegel,* ed. Carl J. Friedrich (New York: Modern Library, 1954), pp. 16–17.

56. See Norman Birnbaum, ed., *Beyond the Crisis* (London: Oxford University Press, 1977).

57. John Schaar, "Legitimacy in the Modern State," in *Power and Community,* ed. P. Green and S. Levinson (New York: Pantheon, 1970); Wilson Carey McWilliams, "On Political Illegitimacy," *Public Policy* 19, 3 (Summer 1971): 430–456.

58. The most interesting Marxist attempt to counter this comes in Maurice Godelier, "System, Structure and Contradiction in *Capital,*" *Structuralism,* ed. M. Lane (New York: Random House, 1967).

59. Weber, *Wissenschaftslehre,* pp. 604–605 (trans. in Gerth and Mills, pp. 148–149). See Strong, *Friedrich Nietzsche and the Politics of Transfiguration,* chap. 3.

60. Michael Walzer, "Radical Politics and the Welfare State," *Dissent* (January–February 1968); see the discussion by J. Peter Euben "On Walzer's *Obligations,*" *Philosophy and Public Affairs* 3, 3 (Spring 1974): 296 ff.

61. Otto Kirchheimer, "Private Man and Society," *Political Science Quarterly* 81, 4 (March 1966): 24.

62. Kenneth Kenniston, *The Uncommitted* (New York: Delta, 1967); Edgar Z. Friedenberg, *Coming of Age in America* (New York: Random House, 1965).

63. Norman O. Brown, "A Reply to Herbert Marcuse," in Marcuse, *Negations* (Boston: Beacon, 1968), pp. 246–247.

64. See Nietzsche's analysis of "petty pleasures" in *On the Geneal-*

ogy of Morals and my commentary on it in *Friedrich Nietzsche and the Politics of Transfiguration,* chap. 8.

65. David Landes, *Revolution in Time* (Cambridge, Mass.: Harvard University Press, 1983). Carlo Cipolla, *Before the Industrial Revolution* (New York: Norton, 1968); E. P. Thompson, "Time, Work-discipline, and Industrial Capitalism," *Past and Present* 38 (December 1967): 56-97. See the account of his first watch by the character Gletkin in Arthur Koestler, *Darkness at Noon* (New York: Bantam, 1966), pp. 182f.

66. For the most sanguine account, see Bennett Berger, *The Survival of a Counterculture* (Berkeley: University of California Press, 1981).

67. The best defense and celebration of modernity is Marshall Berman, *All That Is Solid Melts into Thin Air: The Experience of Modernity* (New York: Simon and Schuster, 1982).

68. See Ernest Gellner, *Contemporary Thought and Politics* (London: Routledge, 1974) and my review in *Theory and Society* 1, 4 (1974): 503-505.

69. Hermann Kahn, *The Next 200 Years* (New York: Morrow, 1976). See also Ronald Inglehart, *The Silent Revolution: Changing Values and Political Styles Among Western Publics* (Princeton, N.J.: Princeton University Press, 1977).

70. See Strong, *Friedrich Nietzsche and the Politics of Transfiguration,* chap 8; Hannah Arendt, *Willing* (New York: Harcourt, Brace, Jovanovich, 1978).

71. Herbert Marcuse, *One Dimensional Man* (Boston: Beacon, 1964).

72. This is Nietzsche's and even Marx's understanding.

73. Søren Kierkegaard, *The Journals of Søren Kierkegaard,* ed. A. Dru (New York: Harper, 1959), p. 97.

74. Max Weber, "Politics as a Vocation" in *From Max Weber.*

75. See my "Hold on to Your Brains: An Essay in Meta-theory" in *Power and Community,* ed. P. Green and S. Levinson (New York: Pantheon, 1970).

5. POLITICAL THEORY AND THE PAROCHIAL

1. See the discussion of the *Confessions* in Peter Brown, *Augustine of Hippo* (Berkeley: University of California Press, 1967).

2. This is, of course, a reference to the opening of the Preface to the second edition of the *Critique of Pure Reason* (New York: St. Martin's Press, 1965).

3. Is this one of the functions of "Rosebud," as Orson Welles gives it to us in *Citizen Kane*?

4. My vision here draws on Hannah Arendt in *The Human Condition* (Chicago: University of Chicago Press, 1958) and *On Revolution*. See also Zolberg, "Moments of Madness," in *Politics and Society*.

5. I am being outrageous, but I would point to Stanley Cavell, *The Senses of Walden* and George Kateb, *Hannah Arendt* (Totowa, N.Y.: Rowman & Allanheld, 1983) as starting points.

6. Here Leslie Fiedler's classic essay on *Huckleberry Finn* in *An End to Innocence* (Boston: Beacon, 1955), pp. 142–151, catches the additional dimensions very well.

7. On these matters see, Bellah et al., *Habits of the Heart*. On mobility, see Stephan Thernstrom and Richard Sennett, eds., *Nineteenth-Century Cities* (New Haven, Conn.: Yale University Press, 1969). I am conscious of being informed here by F. O. Mathiessen, *American Renaissance* (Oxford: Oxford University Press, 1968).

8. Nathaniel Hawthorne, *The House of the Seven Gables* (New York: E. P. Dutton, 1956), pp. 250–251.

9. Calvin, *Instituts de la religion chrétienne*, IV, chapter 20, par. 2.

10. Samuel Beckett, *Endgame* (New York: Grove Press, 1958).

11. Sherwood Anderson, *Winesburg, Ohio* (New York: Viking, 1963), p. 247.

12. Jean-Luc Nancy, *La communauté desoeuvrée* (Paris: Christian Bourgeois, 1986), p. 16.

13. Herman Melville, *Israel Potter: His Fifty Years of Exile* (Evanston, Ill.: Northwestern University Press, 1982). See Alexander Keyssar, *Mellville's* Israel Potter: *Reflections on the American Dream* (Cambridge, Mass.: Harvard University Press, 1969).

14. Merleau-Ponty, *La prose du monde*, p. 197 [my translation].

15. Nathaniel Hawthorne, *The Blithedale Romance* (New York: Norton, 1978).

16. Kurt Vonnegut, *Mother Night*, Preface (New York: Harper & Row, 1966).

17. Max Weber, *Economy and Society*, p. 975.

18. See the analysis in Karl Löwith, "Marx und Weber," *Gesammelte Abhandlungen. Zur Kritik des geschichtlichen Existenz* (Stuttgart: Kohlhammer, 1960), pp. 1–3.

19. See the discussion in Berman, *All That Is Solid Melts into Thin Air: The Experience of Modernity*, chapter 1.

20. John Winthrop, "A Modell of Christian Charitie," in *Puritan Political Ideas*, ed. E. Morgan (Indianapolis: Bobbs-Merrill, 1965).

21. This argument has also been used about questions like the origin of the Civil War and has been conclusively laid to rest in that regard by Eugene Genovese in *The Political Economy of Slavery* (New York: Vintage, 1965), chapter 1.

22. Michael Walzer, *Exodus and Revolution* (New York: Basic Books, 1985).

23. Ibid., p. 149.

24. In part, this fear explains why I am not attracted so much by the great French sociologists. In a letter of November 6, 1936 to his Danish colleague, S. Ranulf, Marcel Mauss, the great French anthropologist and son-in-law of Emile Durkheim, wrote:

> Durkheim, and after him, the rest of us, we are, I think, the authors of the theory of the authority of collective representation. We simply did not predict that great modern societies, more or less emerged from the Middle Ages, could respond to suggestion as Australian aborigines do to their dances, nor be put into motion by a child's chant. Such a return to the primitive was not something we thought about. We had contented ourselves with a few allusions to crowds, when in fact it is really a completely different matter. We were also content to show that it was in the collective spirit that the individual found his both ground and sustenance for his liberty, for his independence, for his personality and his thought. Basically we never envisaged the extraordinary modern means [for generating collectivity].

Mauss in a subsequent letter (May 8, 1939) to Ranulf adds:

> I think that all of this is a tragedy for us, too strong a verification of things that we wrote about and the proof that we should have sought our proof in evil rather than in good.

Cited by Raymond Aron, *Memoires. 50 ans de réflexion politique* (Paris: Juillard, 1983), p. 71. This point is central to the film by H. J. Syderberg, *Hitler, a Film from Germany.* See Philippe Lacoue-LaGarthes and Jean-Luc Nancy, "The Nazi Myth," *Critical Inquiry* 16, 2 (Winter 1990).

25. Part of my language here is affected by the discussion in Cavell, *The Claim of Reason,* pp. 319 ff.

26. See the very plausible claims for such universals in Melvin Spiro, "Cultural Relativism and the Future of Anthropology," *Cultural Anthropology* 1, 3 (August, 1986): 266 f. I do not, however, share the conclusions that Spiro draws.

27. Cavell, *Must We Mean What We Say?* p. 136. See my discussion in *Friedrich Nietzsche and the Politics of Transfiguration,* pp. 290 ff.

28. Max Weber, "Politics as a Vocation" in *From Max Weber.*

29. My discussion draws heavily on Cavell, *The Claim of Reason,* p. 373.

30. Max Weber, *Economy and Society,* p. 975.

INDEX

193